# Harm reduction, human rights, and cannabis in Canada

Andrew Hathaway

# Harm reduction, human rights, and cannabis in Canada

An ethnographic study of the 'marijuana problem'

**LAP LAMBERT** Academic Publishing

**Impressum/Imprint (nur für Deutschland/ only for Germany)**
Bibliografische Information der Deutschen Nationalbibliothek: Die Deutsche Nationalbibliothek
verzeichnet diese Publikation in der Deutschen Nationalbibliografie; detaillierte bibliografische
Daten sind im Internet über http://dnb.d-nb.de abrufbar.
Alle in diesem Buch genannten Marken und Produktnamen unterliegen warenzeichen-, marken-
oder patentrechtlichem Schutz bzw. sind Warenzeichen oder eingetragene Warenzeichen der
jeweiligen Inhaber. Die Wiedergabe von Marken, Produktnamen, Gebrauchsnamen,
Handelsnamen, Warenbezeichnungen u.s.w. in diesem Werk berechtigt auch ohne besondere
Kennzeichnung nicht zu der Annahme, dass solche Namen im Sinne der Warenzeichen- und
Markenschutzgesetzgebung als frei zu betrachten wären und daher von jedermann benutzt
werden dürften.

Coverbild: www.ingimage.com

Verlag: LAP LAMBERT Academic Publishing GmbH & Co. KG
Dudweiler Landstr. 99, 66123 Saarbrücken, Deutschland
Telefon +49 681 3720-310, Telefax +49 681 3720-3109
Email: info@lap-publishing.com

Herstellung in Deutschland:
Schaltungsdienst Lange o.H.G., Berlin
Books on Demand GmbH, Norderstedt
Reha GmbH, Saarbrücken
Amazon Distribution GmbH, Leipzig
**ISBN: 978-3-8433-5933-7**

**Imprint (only for USA, GB)**
Bibliographic information published by the Deutsche Nationalbibliothek: The Deutsche
Nationalbibliothek lists this publication in the Deutsche Nationalbibliografie; detailed
bibliographic data are available in the Internet at http://dnb.d-nb.de.
Any brand names and product names mentioned in this book are subject to trademark, brand
or patent protection and are trademarks or registered trademarks of their respective holders.
The use of brand names, product names, common names, trade names, product descriptions
etc. even without a particular marking in this works is in no way to be construed to mean that
such names may be regarded as unrestricted in respect of trademark and brand protection
legislation and could thus be used by anyone.

Cover image: www.ingimage.com

Publisher: LAP LAMBERT Academic Publishing GmbH & Co. KG
Dudweiler Landstr. 99, 66123 Saarbrücken, Germany
Phone +49 681 3720-310, Fax +49 681 3720-3109
Email: info@lap-publishing.com

Printed in the U.S.A.
Printed in the U.K. by (see last page)
ISBN: 978-3-8433-5933-7

# TABLE OF CONTENTS

## INTRODUCTION

Early twentieth century North America underwent a dramatic shift in the regulation of psychoactive drug use, moving rapidly from an era of unrestricted availability to one of outright prohibition. Since the 1970s or so, new definitions of the "problem" have emerged suggesting drug laws do more harm than the drug use they are intended to prevent. This book takes a closer look at arguments presented from a "constructionist" perspective, with particular attention to the Canadian movement for marijuana law reform. Chapter one examines the debate among constructionists over the meaning of reality and "objectivity" in science. With Alvin Gouldner (1968), I contend that a subjective value commitment is a necessary condition of any objective study. An obligation to concern ourselves with 'solving' social problems furthermore suggests a need to situate claims making in its wider context of culture and social structure (Best 1989, 1993). A contextual reading of constructionist theory frees the analyst to link discursive practices to social arrangements, opening up a whole new body of literature devoted to strategies of critical inquiry in the study of social problems (Gray 1993). To that end, building on Best's (1987) efforts to assess the role of rhetoric in constructing social problems, we briefly touch on politics and social movements research, and the role of the media in claims dissemination and shaping public policy debates.

The second chapter outlines research methods and the problems I encountered in this study of Canadian "public figures" connected to the movement for drug policy reform. Following Malcolm Spector's (1980) work on studying public figures, through analysis of documents and in-depth interviewing designed to generate unique insights and the sharing of information, this research will investigate rhetorical dimensions of the ongoing cannabis debate. A dominant discursive strategy employed, drawing on the rhetoric of substance "harm reduction," is examined in the third chapter, wherein it is described as a preeminently pragmatic, public health response that seeks to mitigate the harms of problematic substance use as opposed to prohibition of the

3

substance use *per se*. Harm reduction measures for cannabis are focused primarily on lowering the social cost of drug laws that have evidently failed to deter its widespread use. By loosening restrictions on possession, it is argued, even partial decriminalization would substantially lower the cost of drug enforcement and mitigate the impact of imposing criminal sanctions. Strategies for minimizing risks to health and safety require additional emphasis on public education efforts to promote less harmful methods of ingestion among regular cannabis users (Morgan, Riley, and Chesher 1993). Yet actively promoting harm reduction still remains highly controversial for medical professionals and treatment service providers.

Harm reduction's claims to pragmatism notwithstanding, the movement has had difficulties influencing social policy due to certain practical and political constraints. As will be explained in the fourth chapter, the compelling language and logic of "harm reduction" is appealing to a wide array of drug abuse practitioners and programs that nonetheless view abstinence as their main objective. Despite its rational appeal, harm reduction ultimately prevents drug law reformers from saying what they mean in support of humane policies (Mugford 1993). Although respect for civil liberties is integral to harm reduction, the acknowledgement of drug use as a basic human right is eschewed in favour of cost-benefit analyses that are claimed to be morally neutral. We are left with a one-sided analysis of cost that undervalues freedom and the benefit of pleasure. By contrast, human rights based arguments for reform are self-consciously political, foremost upholding the power of individual will and self-determination to counter the wildly inaccurate drug-slave analogies of prohibitionists. Disputes over justice in the public realm are treated not as matters for rational inquiry, but rather for the assertion and counterassertion of incompatible sets of premises (MacIntyre 1988). Arguing for change accordingly requires making a choice between rival traditions of argument (Shotter 1993).

Since policy reform opponents carry the authority of established belief, or "presumption" (Czubaroff 1989), conceptual innovation by way of rational reform requires moral grounding in a tradition providing the necessary resources for critical inquiry. By situating arguments for drug law reform within their broader context of philosophical debates and contentions in the liberal tradition, today's policy disputes are recognized as moral problems apt not to be judged against professional standards of rationality. Scientific arguments which deny their own rhetoric are severely disadvantaged in moral debates. In policy disputes over the definition of values and their application, factual evidence is seldom decisive—authoritative judgement and historical precedent often assume far greater importance (Czubaroff 1989). While arguments for drug

4

reform typically concede the immorality of prohibited conduct and then go on to discuss the excessive costs of preventing it, efficiency based arguments have had little success in reducing the scope of criminalized conduct in practice. Where moral judgements remain unchallenged, as with many types of drug use for example, movement toward decriminalization has been negligible (Richards 1982).

The final chapter of this book accordingly examines the grounds on which drug law reform may be viably opposed on the basis of respect for human rights. Lacking adequate expression of personal autonomy as a moral end in and of itself, strictly utilitarian, cost-efficiency assessments are vulnerable to arguments that justify state sanctioned legislation of morality. Demands for drug reform based on empirical analysis of the social costs of law enforcement are thereby secondary to establishing the freedom to use drugs as an individual right. Put otherwise, progressive law reform may thus owe more to advancing moral warrants than to the perfection and diffusion of a harm reduction science. Rational arguments for change notwithstanding, challenging prohibition based on human rights principles requires examination of the context of "the problem" and traditions of moral argument at the core of these debates. An objective of this study, building on the larger emancipatory project of the human sciences, is to facilitate conceptual innovations that contribute to informing critical inquiry.

CHAPTER ONE

**CONSTRUCTIONIST THEORY DEVELOPMENT**

The first chapter looks at major theoretical developments in the sociology of deviance and social problems, and their implications for sociological research. Continuing debates about the nature of "reality" are outlined here with reference to disputes between constructionists and the turn to rhetoric in social constructionism. We begin with a brief history of drug control in Canada prior to overviewing theoretical discussions that inform the present study of drug policy claims making.

**A Brief History of Canada's 'Drug Problem'**[*]

The illicit drug problem in Canada dates to 1908, when the federal government first prohibited the manufacture and sale of smoking opium. For the first time in Canada's history a psychoactive drug had been criminalized, marking a profound shift in drug control policy. In the aftermath of Vancouver's anti-Asiatic riot of 1907, the criminalization of a few thousand, mostly Chinese, opium smokers was an expedient and noncontroversial control measure that passed easily in Parliament. Cocaine was soon added to the schedule of prohibited drugs, and the offence of "illegal drug possession" was introduced to aid police in the enforcement of new drug laws. In 1923 cannabis was summarily included in the schedule by unanimous approval and no debate in the House of Commons. An earlier series of articles in the popular magazine <u>Maclean's</u> had helped to publicly define the drug problem in terms of white fears about a rising tide of immigration to Canada. These racially toned writings by Edmonton magistrate and leading suffragette Emily

---

[*] This section is developed in additional detail in Hathaway, A.D. and Erickson, P.G. 2003. Drug Reform Principles and Policy Debates: Harm Reduction Prospects for Cannabis in Canada. <u>Journal of Drug Issues</u> 33(3): 467-496.

7

Murphy were collected and printed in The Black Candle (1922), a book that informed Canadians about the dangers of drug use by black men using cocaine and the Oriental opium smoker seeking to bring down the "bright browed races of the world." According to Judge Murphy, cocaine and heroin produce delusions rendering the user "insane and dangerous to be at large" (p. 57). Likewise, under the influence of marijuana, addicts to this drug were said to "...become raving maniacs and are liable to kill or indulge in any form of violence to other persons" (p. 333).

In 1923 marijuana use was generally unknown in Canada, and Murphy's claims went widely unchallenged. Whereas the majority of Canadians today know such claims to be wildly inaccurate, there was no alternative view of cannabis consumption at the time. The first reported seizures of marijuana did not occur in Canada until 1932, and House records from the 1920's indicate that many Members of Parliament had never even heard of cannabis. Canada's early history of cannabis prohibition might thus been called the making of a "law without a problem" (Giffen, Lambert, and Endicott 1991). Nevertheless, between 1908 and 1923 the recreational use of cannabis and certain other drugs was effectively transformed from a matter of private indulgence to one of public evil (Boyd 1991). Marijuana, opium and cocaine were elevated to the status of a social problem, their use deserving of severe penalty. A new class of crime had been created, one that would go largely unchallenged for nearly fifty years.

In May of 1972, after three years of public hearings and extensive research on the issue, a government inquiry into the "non-medical use of drugs" (LeDain 1972) recommended removing the criminal penalties prohibiting simple possession of cannabis. The LeDain Commission's proposal was immediately rejected by the government of Canada (Erickson and Smart 1980) and, despite ongoing calls for law reform, forty years later the legislative stalemate continues unresolved.

**Deviance and Social Problems Theory**
Alfred Lindesmith's (1947) early criticism of criminal sanctions against heroin addicts in the United States was only a prelude to the erosion of consensus over drug control that began in the 1950's. Naive versions of consensus theory, defining drug use and other deviance in terms of an assumed common value system, were supplanted by a new orientation that defined deviance as a relative matter of societal definition. "Labeling theory" reoriented the sociology of deviance from the study of rule-breaking behaviour to that of "secondary deviance" (Lemert 1951), with emphasis

8

on processes of becoming deviant and social roles determined by societal reactions. Howard Becker's (1953, 1955) classic work on marijuana offered an explanation for illicit substance use within a framework that was just like any other learning process. He argued deviance is learned in the process of interaction within intimate personal groups.

Following publication of Becker's Outsiders (1963), the sociology of deviance resounded with research from a labeling perspective that described the role of social control agencies in 'amplifying' deviance. A more liberal conception of deviant behaviour, winning sympathy and tolerance for the deviant as one more "sinned against than sinning," spawned a growth of studies in the 1960's on the institutionalized mistreatment of drug users (e.g., Schur 1964; Lindesmith 1965, 1968) and other perpetrators of "victimless" crime (Schur 1965). Towards the end of the decade, however, the liberal agenda of mainstream sociology came under attack by the adherents of a self-styled "radical" school of social theory. Becker and other sociologists with liberal ideologies were disparaged by the new radicals for identifying with "underdogs," thereby promoting a "man-on-his-back" view of deviance (Gouldner 1968), a so-called sociology of "nuts, sluts, and perverts" (Liazos 1973). Sociologists should concern themselves with the study of "political deviance," argued Gouldner, with people fighting back against oppressive institutional arrangements that are otherwise taken for granted.

By 1969 a sociology of criminal law anticipating the political and intellectual ferment of the 1970's was already emerging in the United States and Canada (see Chambliss 1969, Quinney 1969, Turk 1969, Cook 1969). This new generation of conflict theorists rejected the liberal notion of law as a negotiated balance of interests. In the words of Richard Quinney (1969, pp. 25-29): "Law does not represent the compromise of the diverse interests in society, but supports some interests at the expense of others...In the conflict-power model of interest structure...politically organized society is held together by conflicting elements and functions according to the coercion of some segments by others." In light of contemporary changes in industrial society, the "pluralist" conception of conflict played down the Marxian emphasis on ownership of the means of production to account for the emergence of power based on authority in governmental, religious, and other institutional structures.

Notwithstanding their assertions that those with economic power are not necessarily more powerful than authorities in other spheres, pluralists, however, still tended to favour illustrations that demonstrate the influence of economic elites. Amid the social unrest of the 1970's, the

9

emphasis on different "segments of society that have the power to shape public policy" (Quinney 1970, p. 17) was often disavowed by conflict theorists on the grounds that this moderate view was weakening their critical focus on the criminal law as a servant of dominant class interests. By the middle of the decade, Quinney (1974, 1975, 1977), Chambliss (1975, 1976) and other American sociologists joined Britain's circle of "new criminologists" (see Taylor, Walton, and Young 1973) in calling for a more critical analysis of crime control under capitalism. Embracing a more radical, traditionally Marxist conceptualization of ruling class power put studying narcotics laws and other crimes of vice beyond the general purview of many conflict theorists. Whereas "critical criminology" (Taylor 1975) is primarily concerned with laws that serve the interests of an economic elite, most drug law studies tend to favour a pluralist conflict explanation.

Studies on the history of American drug control, for example, suggest that moral entrepreneurship (Becker 1963), "status politics" (Gusfield 1963), bureaucratic organizations (Dickson 1968), interracial hostility (Musto 1973, Bonnie and Whitebread 1974, Helmer 1975), and international obligations (Reasons 1974) were all important factors in the law making process. In Canada's most extensive drug law study to date (Giffen, Lambert, and Endicott 1991, p. 557), the authors "...found no evidence of a powerful business elite bringing about narcotic laws to serve its own interests." Rather, the evidence suggests a pluralist understanding of law as being brought about by groups with the power to influence the legislative process and direct it at relatively powerless groups: "The laws are seen more as a reaction to the characteristics of users than to the drugs themselves, though imputed harms from use of the drugs may be important in the justifying ideology" (p. 11). Giffen and his colleagues note that such explanations may be collectively framed in terms of "drug politics theory" (Himmelstein 1978), a substantive orientation that parallels development of the constructionist approach to studying social problems.

**Constructing Social Problems**

Following Spector and Kitsuse (1977), the constructionist approach to social problems directs attention away from "objective" conditions toward the collective processes whereby alleged conditions are defined as social problems. According to strict constructionist precepts, the verification of claims about conditions is irrelevant to the analysis of social problems. Seeking instead to explain "...how categories of social problems and deviance are produced, and how methods of social control are institutionally established" (Spector and Kitsuse 1977, p. 72),

10

constructionist analyses focus on the "claims-making" activities of different groups as they seek to assert their own definitions of social problems. Since social problems are possible only as assemblages of members' perspectives, strict constructionists take a methodological stance emphasizing a fundamental distinction between the members' practical project and the theoretical project of the sociologist. Most importantly, they must refrain from tacitly privileging their own versions of the condition in question.

Whereas social constructionists are often careful to identify claims about alleged conditions as the proper subject of analysis, however, it has been noted that constructionist explanations generally assume some objective knowledge of the nature of social conditions as unchanging phenomena (Woolgar and Pawluch 1985). Attempts to bracket off the subject's practical project, fostering the Weberian ideal of a purely objective "value-free" social science, predate the emergence of social constructionism of course, and will no doubt continue to challenge the existence and growth of the more openly interpretive "constructivist" (Schwandt 1994) approaches to inquiry. The myth of a value-free social science clearly endures amid the unshakable rhetoric of rationality that is the legacy of our technocratic age. On the other hand, however, unthinking rejection of the value-free myth, outside of the framework of a larger humanistic understanding, breeds complacency about the very values obscured by our technical versions of truth.

As noted by Gouldner (1968), purely technical approaches to "objectivity," employing fixed operational definitions in pursuit of "validity" and "reliability," only tell us what we must do to justify a finding as objective. They tell us nothing about what objectivity means conceptually. For Gouldner, the value commitments of sociologists are not merely inescapable facts of nature; rather, they are a necessary condition of their objectivity. When we talk about the bias or objectivity of a sociologist we are, in effect, talking about the sociologist as if he were a "judge" who must do justice in conformity with some stated normative standard, or value. Objectivity is thus a moral struggle over value commitments, and the grounds for those commitments, that requires explication, for we cannot be objective about the world outside without first knowing ourselves and understanding that such knowledge is always problematic.

The constructionist perspective, defining social problems as claims making activities in which imputed social conditions are merely the subjects of claims, shares much with Gouldner's understanding of the subjective nature of objective reality. For social constructionists, science itself is little more than a perspective, a way of seeing, in which objectivity, or fact, "...is so heavily

11

intertwined with 'understanding,' with the cultural apparatuses of conceptualization, that it can only be assumed to be problematic in any particular instance" (Gusfield 1981, p. 192). In Gusfield's analysis of scientific rhetoric in the construction of the "drinking-driving problem" in America, for example, he notes the political implications of sociology as a "perspective of perspectives," holding up that which is taken for granted as something strange and problematic. He argues: "To find alternative ways of seeing phenomena is to imagine that things can be otherwise...This cannot but be a diminution of the legitimacy which authority gains from a belief in its facticity. When the sociologist is so operating, he presents a world that is political rather than a world of technical necessity" (p. 193).

Arguing that the seemingly unattached, technical language of science serves to hide from recognition that moral and political choices are being made, Gusfield favours the use of "reflexive irony" as a way for the sociologist to stay uncommitted and sceptical of all perspectives, thereby fostering the development of many perspectives. In striving to uphold analytical purity, Gusfield (1981, p. 193) is less supportive of the politically active, or "utopian," sociologist who "...presumes some reality, some perspective that is better than other perspectives." Whereas we are invited to question the notion of scientific objectivity as merely another rhetorical claim serving vested political interests, the strict constructionist must nevertheless strive to maintain his or her godlike "Olympian" detachment from politics and other practical matters. Gouldner (1968) argues, on the contrary, that the partiality of interests which is disavowed by Gusfield is not only unavoidable but necessary for a truly objective understanding of social reality.

For Gouldner, to perpetuate the myth of a value-free social science is as disingenuous as it is injurious to sociology as an intellectual endeavour. In failing to explicate the sentiments and value commitments, including the grounds for those commitments, that inevitably guide our research, we invite complacency by allowing unspoken ideologies to go unexamined. In keeping with the spirit of the late 1960's, Gouldner (1968, p. 111) and other self-confessed radical sociologists wanted to study society's "power elites" and their master institutions, "...with a view to understanding how some are crushed by certain institutions, and how all alike are subjected to institutions that do not permit them to live as they wish." Advocating a kind of "objective partisanship" set within the framework of a larger humanistic understanding, Gouldner railed against so-called "liberal" sociology for its blind alliance with the upper bureaucracy of the welfare state.

12

Charges of value complacency and collusion with authorities by liberal social scientists today coexist alongside very different accusations, where 'well-heeled' academics more often are disparaged by status quo defenders for their role in undermining political stability for the sake of personal politics. Yet, despite the general view that sociologists tend to work from "left-liberal" assumptions that are manifested in their research, surprisingly little has been written by those so charged in defense of liberal ideologies. The spectre of value-free science is essential to continuation of the misappropriation and disavowal of liberalism as an ideological label. Accordingly, extending Gouldner's call for more attention to objective partisanship within a humanistic framework, much of the following discussion is devoted to employing the liberal tradition as a strategy demanding more open and articulated rhetorical development in today's drug policy debates. To that end, the emergence of constructionism's focus on claims making in the context of contemporary western culture is discussed below with reference to work by Best (1989) and Gusfield (1985) and other theoretical developments.

## Social Problems in Cultural Context

As noted by Woolgar and Pawluch (1985), despite programmatic claims that adhere to relativism, constructionists generally assume some 'objective' knowledge of conditions in their studies—a consequence of which are lapses into realism in their social problems explanations. In response, the "strict" constructionists reemphasized the need to avoid making assumptions about objective conditions, in order to live up to the analytical ideal of a purely "definitional perspective" (see Schneider 1985a, Spector and Kitsuse 1987). Among the prominent constructionists of the mid-1980's, only Gusfield (1985, p. 17) openly challenged strict constructionism's "preoccupation with the logic of theory" at the expense of empirical scrutiny. By the end of the decade, however, the need to make some assumptions about social problems conditions was increasingly acknowledged by constructionists.

Best (1989) has characterized this "weaker," more pragmatic standpoint as "contextual constructionism," a position owing much to the interactionist perspective in its approach to studying the empirical world. In the words of Herbert Blumer, the preeminent scholar in the conceptual development of symbolic interactionism: "The task of social and psychological sciences is to improve human judgement—not to supply fixed rules, laws, or rigid generalizations. The need is for relevant and usable information—and the cultivation of abilities to use the information intelligently" (cited in Becker 1988, p. 21). Although they retain a primary focus on the process of claims making, and do not necessarily concern themselves with the accuracy of claims or the actual social conditions about which they are made, most constructionists have opted to study social problems within their wider context of culture and social structure. Claims and studies about claims are inseparable from the context in which they are produced (Rafter 1992).

Recognizing that knowledge is always relative, that the meanings of all things have a situational base, contextual analyses of social problems seek to break out of the narrow circle of claimants assertions to understand the meaning of these claims within the context in which they are collectively produced. Notwithstanding recognition that "...social problems lie in and are the products of a process of collective definition" (Blumer 1971, p. 301), the strict constructionist approach to social problems is restricted by insisting we achieve the distance needed to focus purely on the process of collective definition—rather than unknowingly participating in it. An agenda such as this can only be achieved at the expense of empirical knowledge and scrutiny of the objective makeup of social problems, which "...should be sought as a corrective for ignorance or misinformation concerning this objective makeup" (Blumer 1971, p. 305).

The analyst must seek knowledge about social conditions that can help to explain why certain claims emerge when they do, taking note of discrepancies between claims and other knowledge about conditions (Best 1989). Since other sources of knowledge about conditions are also social constructions, these too are to be treated as claims in their own right. A contextual reading of constructionist theory that recognizes culture and its representations thereby frees the analyst to link discursive practices to social arrangements, opening up new literature to social problems theorists and corresponding strategies of critical inquiry (Gray 1993). Gusfield's (1981) argument that even the scientific evidence used to support claims about social problems should be seen as part of the claims makers' efforts to persuade has gained a steady foothold in constructionist debates.

Consequently, the constructionist project has evolved as an emerging theory of "social problems discourse," the aim of which is to identify the rhetorical styles and strategies that are "conventional features of the claims making process" (Ibarra and Kitsuse 1993, p. 25), and to document through case studies the broader role of rhetoric in social problems construction (e.g., Best 1987). Ibarra and Kitsuse (1993, p. 29), still striving to preserve the integrity of a purely definitional perspective, stress that the strict constructionist never leaves language; thus they

14

oppose the development of discrete theories through case studies "...on the social construction of X, Y, and Z." Less committed to the logic of constructionism, Best (1993, p. 118) accepts that while "...case studies inevitably violate the guidelines for strict constructionism," sociologists should nonetheless remain committed to the process of empirical investigation with the goal of building "grounded theory" (Glaser and Strauss 1967) through qualitative methods of analytical induction.

In sum, it has been argued that despite the logical desirability of strict constructionism, its proponents have acknowledged the inherent difficulty of sustaining any method that would be consistent with the requirements of a purely definitional approach. Sarbin and Kitsuse (1994, p. 14), for example, have conceded that "...investigators and analysts in spite of themselves cannot help but import their interests, if not their professional agendas, into their interactions with their informants." Unlike many earlier adherents proselytizing on the virtues of a value-free approach to social science, strict constructionists have acknowledged that their vision of an "assumption-free" sociology is an illusory, unattainable goal (Best 1995). In this light, Best (1995, p. 348) has argued that "...by default, all constructionist analysis becomes a form of contextual constructionism."

The notion that sociologists must neither presume any knowledge nor attempt to assess members' definitions of objective social conditions too narrowly construes the constructionist project. Upholding the logic of theory over the exercise of analytical scrutiny, strict constructionists insist on asking the same questions about each claims making campaign rather than focusing on the interesting features of a particular case, and are thereby precluded from exercising the dogged analytical scrutiny that comprises the sociological imagination. For constructionism to be of any practical use, it must concern itself with all knowledge about conditions that may be applied to the study of social problems. The cultural context of claims not only situates them structurally, it renders them meaningful for political purposes in a world where social scientists, like the people they study, should be free to challenge our taken-for-granted institutional arrangements.

To maintain the foregoing emphasis on value commitment and the importance of evaluative freedom in the sociological endeavour, an explicit goal of this research is the advancement of constructionist theory as an analytical framework for studying and informing the drug reform debate. With particular reference to the growing controversy over prohibitionist responses to the 'marijuana problem,' the aim is to delineate the dominant styles and strategies of

15

drug reform rhetoric as critical tools for development in challenging outmoded punitive drug policies. As a prelude to discussion of the context of debate and associated strategies of drug reform claims making, the constructionist turn to rhetoric and social problems discourse is examined with an eye to central sensitizing concepts, and related insights of analytical importance.

### The Constructionist Turn to Rhetoric

Use of scientific knowledge as a strategy of argument in social problems claims making, notes Gusfield, is associated with shifts over time towards a more rational style of public discourse. To illustrate, he points out the legitimating role of science in shaping the official definition of drug problems: "The rules of the game now demand that ideas be set forth in the language and tactics of rational debate and analysis in terms of public rather than private interests. The participants must appear to be rational and informed persons, and they must persuade rather than influence the listeners. It is a game of persuasion. The expert assumes importance in this game because he or she assumed an informed and impartial position. As knowledge is disseminated, it sets limits to the public acceptability of ideas" (Gusfield 1975, p. 13). The impartiality of science, one might argue, is routinely questioned by sophisticated audiences today. However, experts in the drug field have successfully challenged the factual basis for public policies and are "deeply subversive," insofar as they function "...to break down the public appearance of a united and consensual society on the question of drug use" (p. 12).

The expected level of public discourse has shifted to the point where the lurid prohibitionist claims of the past are increasingly inappropriate in the contemporary context of rational debate. Nonetheless, as noted in Canadian experience, recommended changes based on scientific scrutiny of longstanding evidence has had negligible impact on the course of public policy. Despite the credibility of science and objectivity, it is as true today as at the time Gusfield (1975) observed that "...knowledge makes less difference than conventional theory will admit." In the arena of drug politics, and likely any social problem, "...scientific knowledge is only one of a number of factors that bear upon the symbolic and instrumental character of official public action" (p. 13). Extending Gusfield's focus on the rhetoric of science, Best (1987) explored the ways that values become incorporated into claims, aiming to assess the broader role of rhetoric in social problems construction. Whereas constructionists generally acknowledge that claims may be grounded in values, they concentrate mainly on social organizational factors—that is, the process of claims

16

making and people who make claims—rather than the claims themselves.

In their original statement of the social problems perspective, Spector and Kitsuse (1977) warn against trying to explain claims making based on the values of claims makers. Although it is clearly understood that in claims making campaigns "...values are one of the resources members use in their efforts to define conditions as social problems" (p. 96), constructionist case studies often seem to treat the claims themselves as a given (Best 1987). Approaching claims making in terms of its culture rather than its organization *per se*, Best (1995, p. 8) shifts our attention to the construction and presentation of claims, seeking to describe the ways social problems are "typified" by claims makers. Accordingly, he notes that: "Typification occurs when claimsmakers characterize a problem's nature.... Claimsmakers inevitably characterize problems in particular ways: They emphasize some aspects and not others, they promote specific orientations, and they focus on particular causes and advocate particular solutions."

In his analysis of the rhetorical construction of the missing children problem in America, Best (1987) groups typifying statements by claims makers into three main categories—grounds, warrants, and conclusions (see also Toulmin 1958). He argues claims about social problems are not to be taken for granted; rather, claims are conclusions that must first be established by claims makers. Statements about grounds are the foundation for claims that serve to define or interpret a problem, giving the problem a particular orientation, setting its boundaries, and suggesting appropriate avenues for response. Once the human dimensions of a problem are established, claims makers usually try to assess the range and magnitude of the problem as one that extends throughout society affecting many innocent victims who cannot be ignored. Grounds statements thereby establish the basic "facts" about a problem through specific examples, usually selected for their extreme and emotive nature, that provide a suitable reference for discussions of the problem in general and tend to suggest a clear or inevitable conclusion, typically a call to action to solve the putative problem.

While in Best's scheme grounds statements provide the foundation for claims and point towards certain solutions, effective warrants are essential, for it is statements about warrants that justify drawing conclusions from the grounds that are established. He argues that whereas disputes over the factual grounds of a claim need not damage one's conclusions, in order for an argument to be persuasive the audience to be persuaded must ordinarily belong to a field or discipline that deems the warrant valid. Accordingly, Best (1987, p. 109) notes that: "While it is relatively easy to

17

debate the merits of grounds statements, it is more difficult to defend a warrant which one's audience refuses to validate." Since it is in the warrant that values most often come into play, he further states that, depending on the nature and receptivity of the target audience, there are often very good reasons to gloss over warrants. As a result warrants are often kept implicit in public discourse, and are commonly tailored to persuade particular audiences belonging to different argument fields.

Most importantly, regardless of the factual foundation of a claim or the field of argument engaged, viable claims, contends Best (1987, p. 114-115), always have compelling warrants: "If grounding claims in examples is commonplace, finding convincing warrants is essential. Warrants bridge the gap between grounds and conclusions. An audience might accept a claims-maker's version of a problem without adopting the recommended policies. Warrants, through references to values and interests, justify solutions." Claims making is a rhetorical activity that inevitably involves selecting from available arguments, and emphasizing those arguments that are deemed persuasive in a given field or discipline. As participants in the social problems process address new audiences and are able to assess the response to their claims, the claims may be revised and reconstructed over time in the hopes of making them more persuasive. Once again, since all knowledge is disseminated, rhetorical decisions are an integral part of the claims making process, and all such decision making is necessarily dependent on the cultural context of claims.

With regard to what they call "vernacular constituents" of social problems discourse, Ibarra and Kitsuse (1993) caution against the single social condition emphasis of the contextual perspective, and against constructionist's typically unspoken tendency to objectify condition categories. Insisting on strict compliance with the constructionist emphasis on language and definitional processes, the authors advocate a more general, and theoretically removed, focus on the "symbolically demarcated social realities" that mediate conventional ways of speaking. If the constructionist ideal calls for suspending the "natural attitude," researchers must not tacitly be using the vernacular resources that should be assembled as data for theoretical construction. Yet the authors readily acknowledge that "...the issues posed by rhetorical strategies, motifs, and styles are particularly context sensitive" (p. 49). The rhetorical styles and strategies used by claims makers are situated in moral universes and settings that inevitably contribute to the way the social problems process proceeds.

In the contemporary context of rational debate, the scientific style is difficult to distinguish from other styles of discourse. That is, the disinterested style of scientific rhetoric, which assumes that "the facts" of the case are objective and discoverable, is routinely coopted as scientists' disagreements about "scientific claims" become the disagreements of participants in the social problems process (Aronson 1984). The frustration among experts, who strive fruitlessly to make rationality relevant to drug policy debates, has for some time been a source of commentary (e.g., Blumstein 1993, Erickson 1998). Despite the claims of scientists, debates surrounding drug laws in the US, Canada, and other "rational societies" (Gould 1994) are ordinarily decided in terms of temperance ideology or dominant values manifested in our legal institutions, and widely propagated in mainstream media and other cultural forums in which social problems are constructed. A more in-depth analysis of claims dissemination and the shaping of claims making through the agency of media is beyond our scope here; but the rise of media studies, and interest in social movements, in the sociology of deviance is nonetheless noteworthy for its relevance to theory.

## Politics, Social Movements, and the Role of the Media

Gamson (1992) argues cultural meanings are negotiated through media discourse, wherein spotlighted "facts" take on meaning by being framed in some way while ignoring other ways. Western society has long upheld the political ideal of the democratic distribution of knowledge, assuming rational dialogue and an informed public engaging in discussion through a diverse array of media. However, media studies have revealed inherent limits to political dialogue in news media and its role in reproducing hegemonic power relations (Ericson, Baranek, and Chan 1987). In our increasingly "administered society" the media reflects the dominant ideology, working to providing a stable "symbolic canopy" (Berger and Luckmann 1966) in the face of cultural pluralism. The concept of "moral panics" was popularized for its description of the role of mainstream media in maintaining the status quo. Although morality provides a context for the content of the panic, a plurality of interests better help explain its timing (Goode and Ben-Yehuda 1994).

Many studies have suggested a collusion between media and law enforcement, reinforcing status quo assumptions on drug control through fear mongering about the harms of drug use (e.g., Gusfield 1981; Reeves and Campbell 1994; Reinarman 1988; Reinarman and Levine 1995). More recently the idea of moral panic was suggested to require revising to reflect the expansion of the media and greater number of participants engaging in debate (McRobbie and Thornton 1995). In our "multi-mediated" social world, today's "folk devils" are defended in the same mass media that scolds them, and even find their lifestyles being actively promoted through their own alternative micro-media resources. Notwithstanding the resilience of media driven panics and exaggerated claims about the latest 'epidemic,' in the last two decades we have witnessed a dramatic increase in media coverage of opposing views on drugs. The advent of the World Wide Web put drug policy subversive information at the fingertips of millions; and mass media increasingly has opened up a forum for serious debate about drug issues and exposure to arguments for liberal reform.

To demonstrate the growth in mainstream media attention to the drug debate in Canada throughout the 1990s, up to 1997 there were more cannabis related news items listed in the Canadian Periodical Index than for the previous three decades combined. Most notably, between 1996 and '97, news stories about marijuana more than doubled; and a 1997 survey of drug coverage that sampled over 1300 columns and newspaper editorials, revealed that 82% were advocating for some degree of liberal drug policy reform (Fraser Institute 1997). Investigative news programs and editorials that call for changes most especially to marijuana laws since the 1990s have continued to appear in media covering the full spectrum of political opinion. Clearly, sociological descriptions of the media's role in designating deviance—for example, by instigating panics that reinforce existing hegemonic definitions of drug problems—require some adaptation in light of these developments.

The reality of dealing with social difference in pluralistic, heterogeneous societies means that moral panics are not necessarily hegemonic, but rather continually contested societal constructions (McRobbie and Thornton 1995). With increasing media literacy, social differentiation, and segmentation among audiences, moral relativity now dominates the landscape in today's social problems arenas. According to Gamson (1992), social movements are founded on cultural themes rather than "values." Unlike values, cultural themes are dialectical in nature. For every theme there is a countertheme; "...whenever one is invoked the other is always present in latent form, ready to be activated with the proper cue" (p. 135). Counterthemes are adversarial by nature and typically challenge some specific aspect of the mainstream culture, thereby providing an entry point for collective action. Social movements seeking to legitimate formally deviant behaviours, for example, are mobilized to attack dominant cultural codes on what is normal. This mandate is explicit in the case of NORML (the National Organization for the Reform of Marijuana

20

Laws), a lobby group whose acronym calls for social changes that go beyond revisiting the marijuana laws.

Political consciousness is forged in the process of collective action and the most likely context, or frame, for that action is a threat to the pattern of people's everyday lives. Gamson (1992) discusses three components of the "collective action frames" that are manifested in social movements: injustice, agency, and identity. The *identity* component refers to the process of defining a "we" in opposition to some "they" who have different values or interests, and *agency* refers to the consciousness that it is possible to alter policies or conditions through collective action. The *injustice* component refers to the moral indignation expressed through a political consciousness that supports collective action. Although injustice seems to be the key integrating factor insofar as it implies the possibility of change, in the absence of any of these factors the process will take longer and is more likely to be aborted. The possibility of change is thereby enhanced by combining resources to construct an issue frame that is both anchored in personal understandings and linked to broader cultural themes.

Whereas media discourse is a predominantly cultural resource, its images are infused with both cultural and personal meanings. Garnered through experiential knowledge and popular wisdom based on shared knowledge of what "everyone knows," personal meanings contribute to the framing of issues in certain ways, and are generally constructed in association with a particular subculture rather than the broader culture *per se*. Oppositional subcultures, providing a supportive environment for collective action, are created by people concerned with making lives, not history. A pervasive practical cynicism about politics is commonly manifested in everyday forms of resistance that require little or no planning, involving personal acts of evasion and deception rather than rebellious collective action. Whereas this kind of opposition does have its collective aspects, Gamson (1992, p. 61) notes "...even minimal acceptance of basic assumptions about political reality is enough to discourage most people from participating actively in the political process."

Insofar as the mass media favours actors over context, it shifts the public focus away from social factors towards a concrete target that is often used to channel righteous indignation. Since public knowledge is not limited to that supplied by media, people round out and evaluate news items in accordance with past learning to determine how well the information squares with personal experience. However, the lay public has only indirect access to experts through the agency of media. Most reporting on the marijuana controversy, for example, relies on

21

"...information channelled through individual spokespersons who are more likely to be health-science administrators, or 'celebrity' authorities in tangentially related fields, than the specialists actually conducting relevant research" (Shepherd 1981, p. 135). While public indignation may be used to sustain collective action, the sensationalist bent of media fragments meaning in a way that blurs broader power relations and structural causation. Gamson (1992) suggests there are important class differences affecting people's reliance on dominant media frames.

University educated middle-class consumers are more likely to attend to media discourse in the process of framing issues than to popular wisdom or experiential knowledge. Accordingly, the middle-class may be more affected by shifting media frames, and are perhaps less likely than the lower classes to generate the kind of indignation that is needed to produce injustice frames fuelled by public outrage. Gamson's observations have important implications for social movements, with respect to mobilizing strategies for integrating issue frames and disparate class interests. According to Kingdon (1995), however, mass media is less of an impetus to collective action than a vehicle for magnifying movements already started. While media activity may be inconsequential for those inside political circles, he argues, "going public" can be vitally important to outsiders who challenge social policies or status quo arrangements. For example, Anderson (1981) provides a journalistic account of how, during the mid-1970's, the lobby group NORML capitalized on media contacts through a series of strategic "leaks" to the press that forced the issue of marijuana decriminalization in key political circles.

The same stirring of controversy and moral indignation that is so easily translated into political issues in the US, however, may be more limiting, or even counterproductive, for Canadian social movements. Indeed, it has been argued that public controversies in Canada are commonly used by government to avoid seeking legislative solutions. In her study of political differences between Canada and the United States, Schwartz (1981) found there is a sharper boundary between polity and society in Canada. There are fewer social movements, less single-minded overt partisanship, and less use of the courts as a means of political influence. Whereas American interest groups make every effort at their disposal to influence both the public and the actions of government, Canadian interest groups are more likely to seek compromise through direct orderly contact with government (Pross 1975). Unlike the United States where such issues have been known to establish new boundaries, often blurring the lines between political process and other social concerns, moral causes are generally kept within the confines of customary politics in

22

Canada.

Schwartz (1981) argues that the instruments required for social change are actually quite limited in Canadian politics. Members of the Liberal and New Democratic parties, for example, regularly propose and publicly support liberal reforms in the legal system. But compared to their American counterparts, individual party members are relatively ineffective in shaping the political agenda of parliament. Like many other moral causes in Canada, which tend to be defused through the actions of government agencies purporting to acknowledge the legitimacy of the issue, the marijuana controversy has been less of a political symbol than it has in the United States. As a living remnant of 1960's youth culture, the marijuana reform movement in Canada nonetheless continues with an unabated fervour with no apparent hint of resolution decades later.

Such highly politicized moral causes create similar problems for policy makers regardless of political structure (Schwartz 1981). Whereas policy decisions are rarely based on concern only for evaluation of cost-benefit assessments, the political process generally follows a fairly predictable order. By chronicling events and the actors involved, research on political arenas can provide us with parallel information on how alternatives are considered and policies are made, offering fuller scope for explanation. Without engaging in endless description, or obsessing over the logic of theory, social problems explanations must address the ways problems are framed and embedded in an issue complex, and trace the different paths they take onto the political agenda. Moreover, by attending to process we are reminded that political actions have real consequences, allowing for clarification and criticism on the ways political decisions are made (Schwartz 1986).

## Rhetorical Work:  Patterns and Styles of Expression

It is worth remembering that the political context of social problems—including abstract notions such as the 'political climate' or "national mood" (Kingdon 1995) of the people or times with respect to certain social issues—is part of the larger cultural context in which viable social movements must learn to mobilize to generate and maintain public support. Just as people's decisions to make claims emerge from a larger cultural context, so do their rhetorical choices. Best (1987, p. 117) argues: "Claims-makers articulate their claims in ways which they find (and believe their audiences will find) persuasive. The larger cultural context—the weight assigned to various sorts of evidence, the relative importance given to different values, current standards for appropriate social policies, and the degree of consensus about these various judgments—affects

23

rhetorical work." He goes on to identify several general patterns of rhetorical work required to construct persuasive claims.

Recall that Spector and Kitsuse (1977, p. 96) warned against too much attention to motives and values, for these deflect attention from the organization of claims making toward "...the supposed antecedents of the activity, rather than the activity itself." Accordingly, Best (1987, p. 117n) argues, "...many constructionist studies seem to posit that claims-making emerges from a constant pool of potentially articulatable claims." The pervasive sense of uncertainty in rhetorical work is often overlooked in case studies, which tend to focus more directly on the processes of resource mobilization that have lead to successful claims making campaigns. Accordingly, further to interests or motives and the mobilization of resources as a means to effective claims making, Best (1987) emphasizes social problems "ownership" as central to constructionist analyses of rhetoric.

When studying rhetorical frames and strategies based on ownership, it is generally understood that well-established social problems are owned by well-established claims makers. Whereas those inside political circles have easy access to policy makers, political outsiders who challenge status quo arrangements must attempt to reach and persuade the general public to pressure policy makers. Since it is ordinarily in the best interest of policy makers to delay taking action, to wait for an accommodating shift in public opinion, the early stages of rhetorical work are primarily comprised of demands for interpretive change, for the audience to acknowledge or adopt a new orientation to a problem, and to justify viewing the problem in a different way. Demands for reinterpretation are commonly propelled by outrage and directed at an already converted or openly hostile audience during the early stages of social problem construction. Because inexperienced political outsiders must attempt to appeal to 'the people'—and must therefore attract media attention with 'newsworthy' stories featuring novelty, sensation, and conflict—the most appropriate claims are usually the most straightforward, often emphasizing "rectitude" or moral uprightness as a central rhetorical theme.

The rhetoric of rectitude is ideal for bringing new problems to public attention (Schneider 1985b). But experienced claims makers, operating on the inside of political circles to redefine well-established social problems, tend to move toward a rhetoric of rationality developed from principles established in earlier campaigns. In Best's (1987, pp. 116-117) words: "Experienced claims-makers, operating in well-developed social movements, usually favor the rhetoric of rationality. These claims-makers often can maneuver from a beachhead of accepted principles established during earlier campaigns for reinterpretation. Their later campaigns tend to feature more detailed agendas for policy changes, as well as a clearer sense of which items—whether out of principle or pragmatism—deserve priority. The audience is likely to be seen as persuadable, so that a rhetoric of rationality lets the claims-maker negotiate successful advances. Here, the demands tend to be for action; a rhetoric of rationality is more likely to be invoked to shape policy."

As further noted by Best, the foregoing dichotomy cannot but oversimplify the reality of claims making by failing to do justice to the complicated character of claims makers' demands and their audiences. Since rhetorical work inevitably involves choosing to emphasize the claims deemed most persuasive in light of their larger cultural context, it is important to stress that most claims incorporate both moral and rational themes. To reiterate, while warrants or values justifying drawing conclusions from grounds are often glossed over in claims making campaigns, compelling warrants are crucial to the validation of socially viable claims. According to Ibarra and Kitsuse (1993), rhetorical idioms refer to the distinctive ways in which the problematic status of conditions is elaborated through moral vocabularies providing participants with sets of themes that endow their claims with significance. Rhetorical idioms render claims both symbolically coherent and morally competent, usually positing "...hierarchies of value (e.g., freedom over oppression) with which it is difficult to disagree without discrediting oneself" (p. 38). Countering claims thereby requires a certain artfulness in the selection and use of vernacular resources.

Alternative rhetorical idioms perform an important service in counter claims making. Idioms other than the ones implicit in a claim are particularly useful for shifting the focus of discourse singled out by the claimant to the meaning of the claims making itself. Describing the counter-rhetorical strategies commonly employed to redefine America's drug problem, Ibarra and Kitsuse (1993) note that the "war on drugs" initiated under the Reagan and Bush administration in the 1980's was rendered problematic when civil libertarians, countering prohibitionist claims rooted in the "rhetoric of endangerment," invoked a "rhetoric of entitlement" based on individual rights to privacy and freedom of expression. The rhetoric of entitlement is egalitarian in its aversion to forms of discrimination against categories of people, and stems from a relativist philosophy that emphasizes the fundamental importance of protecting human rights to expressivity, liberty, and equal justice for all.

Ibarra and Kitsuse (1993, p. 34, italics in original) describe the critical features of the entitlement frame as follows: "...*lifestyle, diversity, choice, tolerance, empowerment,* and so forth. *Liberation* evokes the value of having the freedom to choose how one might realize one's life...claimants seek to expand the distribution or scope of a good, service, or right. The notion is that the greater the extension of *fair play, tolerance, justice, equality before the law, respect for human dignity,* etc., into greater spheres of social life, the greater the benefits for all members of the society." The authors note further that the rhetorical idiom of entitlement is commonly associated with the counter-rhetorical strategy of "perspectivizing," a mundane form of relativism that characterizes claims as opinions, or matters of perspective, to which claimants are entitled, while implying that these need not be shared by the counterclaimant, and nor need their policy directives.

Claimants who insist such relativizing reflects a lack of moral competence may thereby open themselves up to charges of intolerance; "...this rhetoric is being employed whenever counterclaimants make reference to 'life-style' as a legitimation of a series of activities: That the condition in question is a life-style is supposed to guarantee its propriety" (Ibarra and Kitsuse 1993, p. 40). 'Moral relativism,' as both an argument in favour of maintaining status quo arrangements and as a principle upheld by many policy reformers promoting norms of tolerance and individual autonomy, is discussed at greater length in a later chapter. Here it is sufficient to note that the counter-rhetoric of moral perspectivizing is a common strategy for overcoming marginality. Insofar as counterclaimants to the drug war often sidestep moral questions, undermining rather than enhancing their credibility as participants in social problems discourse, "...by studying counterrhetorics we can discern how credibility is sustained by virtue of being well-versed in the vernacular" (Ibarra and Kitsuse 1993, p. 43).

In the context of rational public debate, the recurrent drug war theme of endangerment—typically featuring fear provoking characterizations of drug abuse as being a crisis of 'epidemic' proportions—is increasingly vulnerable to the "counterrhetoric of hysteria," a way of speaking aimed at deproblematizing exaggerated claims through the assumption that "...the moral judgement of the claimants is not based in a 'sound' assessment of the condition but is under the influence of 'irrational' or 'emotional' factors" (p. 42). Ibarra and Kitsuse (1993) classify this strategy as an example of unsympathetic counter-rhetoric, that which approves neither the characterization of the problem nor the proffered remedy. Sympathetic counter-rhetorics differ insofar as they accept, in whole or in part, the problematic status of conditions but not the suggested remedies. Consistent with the liberal stance of drug reformers seeking to initiate change within the system, their rhetorical strategies exemplify the experienced 'insider' style of sympathetic criticism.

Ibarra and Kitsuse (1993, p. 41) observe, for example: "Tactical critics accept the characterization of the condition-category being proffered, but...suggest that the means claimants are employing might themselves be viewed and treated as a social problem....Of all sympathetic counterrhetorical moves, this one carries the possibility of being seen as the least hostile by claimants, for the 'counterclaimant' is both sympathetic with the effort to problematize *and* is willing to discuss tactics. Whereas the rhetoric of entitlement is most naturally applied in instances of injustice or threats to personal freedom, the drug war rhetoric of endangerment, ordinarily delivered in a scientific style of reasoning endorsed by medical testimony, reinforces official definitions of the 'drug problem' in terms of a threat to the health and safety of the human body. Ibarra and Kitsuse (1993, p. 35, italics in original) also note that "...inasmuch as the presumption is that individuals have the *right* to be safe from harm, to have good health, and to be shielded from preventable or reducible types of bodily risk," the rhetoric of endangerment is a relative of entitlement discourse.

The moral urgency of the former is due less to issues of freedom and equality, however, than to optimal health and bodily function. The authors argue further: "The rhetoric of endangerment shifts the site to which urgent action must attend...where the rhetoric of entitlement evokes the fundamental importance of expressivity, the rhetoric of endangerment...concerns recommend weighing the value of expressivity against the risks posed by expressive practices and beliefs....Positive terms address the hope that has been evoked: *hygiene, prevention, nutritiousness, fitness,* and so on. Negative terms pinpoint the processes that warrant fear: *disease, pathology, epidemic, risk, contamination, health threat,* etc." (p. 35). Through the strategic shifting of moral discourse themes, the rhetoric of rationality and its logical counterpart, the "rhetoric of unreason" (Ibarra and Kitsuse 1993)—emphasizing the importance of informed decision making regarding one's personal health and safety, and public education as a means of solving the problem—are made readily available to liberal reformers and status quo defenders alike. Thus, despite the tendency to downplay moral warrants and values by adopting modern scientific standards, the study of moral discourse in claims making is intrinsic to any social problems analysis.

**Summary**

The foregoing overview of theoretical developments and the ontological disputes between constructionists has largely favoured a contextual approach to social problems. A contextual reading of constructionist theory frees the analyst to link discursive practices to social arrangements and opens up new critical literature and insights. With Gouldner (1968), I contend that a subjective value commitment is not only unavoidable but necessary for any 'objective' social problems analysis. The language of problem solving further requires that we locate claims making in its context of culture and social structure (Best 1989, 1993). The evolving role of media as a deviance designator and claims disseminator were described with reference to social movements, politics, and culture and the present emphasis on rhetoric.

Best's (1987) dichotomy of moral versus rational styled discourse, and other contributions such as Ibarra and Kitsuse's (1993) work on counter-rhetoric is cited, with specific reference to the study of claims making in the social movement for drug policy reform. The tacit acceptance of endangerment themes in harm reductionist approaches to claims making is examined at some length in the analysis to come. Prior to shedding light on its strategic limitations, and the merits of adopting a morally invested, human rights perspective on drug issues, the study methods and some problems I encountered during fieldwork are taken up before in chapter two.

# CHAPTER TWO
## RESEARCH METHODS

Marijuana use in Canada is a widely tolerated lifestyle choice pursued by many otherwise conventional, law-abiding citizens, with few reported adverse consequences (Hathaway 1997a,b). Forty years after the LeDain Commission (1972) findings called for prompt attention to the marijuana laws, the intransigence of punitive drug policies is striking. Consistent with the aforementioned interest in rhetoric, and frustration among experts who have called for law reform, the present focus on claims making by drug policy reformers extends my previous qualitative work on marijuana use to the social problems process as a topic of research. In this chapter, I describe the methodology employed in a study of Canadian drug reform claims making. We look at implications of researching public figures, as well as broader challenges about the defensibility and presentation of evidence from qualitative field work.

### The Study

The focus of this research is on rhetoric employed by claims makers seeking to redefine the official status of marijuana. Neglect in the sociological literature on the strategies of experts and other advocates to influence drug control policy justifies adopting an exploratory approach. Accordingly, my intent is to work toward a grounded theory of drug reform discourse following the usual canons and procedures set out by Glaser and Strauss (1967), including open coding, theoretical sampling, and the method of constant comparison, treating concepts as the basic units of analysis (see also Corbin and Strauss 1990, Strauss and Corbin 1994). Initial data were collected by means of documentary research to establish central players in the cannabis debate. Data gathered from newsletters, brochures, bulletins, and other activities by drug policy organizations were treated as "cultural artifacts" (Jenks 1995) possessing important information about what these groups believe and how they operate. Although the only act of membership for most participants in these organizations consists in writing a check for dues or occasionally reading a newsletter, their views are accessible to scientific study insofar as they actively seek to publicize them.

Following up on names and positions gleaned from sources including statements by experts and activists, court transcripts, and content analysis of various print media, key informants were identified and selected for interviews on the basis of their accessibility, levels of experience, and general involvement in the cannabis debate. Participants are listed, in the order they were interviewed between March and October of 1998:

**Eric Single** is a former Senior Scientist with the Addiction Research Foundation and Professor of Preventative Medicine and Biostatistics at the University of Toronto. Professor Single has published extensively in the areas of alcohol and illicit drug policy issues. He also served as an advisor to the Liquor License Board of Ontario and has been a consultant to the World Health Organization.

**Umberto Iorfida** is the former National Director of the lobby group NORML in Canada. After a period of dormancy in the 1980's, NORML Canada was revived by Iorfida in the 90's. Following a 1992 police raid on his home, he also launched a successful court challenge to section 462.2 of the criminal code banning illicit "drug literature."

**Alan Young** is a Toronto lawyer and Professor at York University's Osgoode Hall Law School. Professor Young gained prominence for his counsel on behalf of hemp activists (helping to obtain the first hemp cultivation license issued in 50 years in Canada) and numerous challenges of the laws prohibiting cannabis for medical and recreational uses. In 1994 he fought successfully to overturn the ban on drug literature (Iorfida v MacIntyre) and later anchored a constitutional challenge (Regina v Clay) of the ban on cannabis in Canada.

**Robert Solomon** is a Professor of Law at the University of Western Ontario. He has been involved in research on drug policy for decades and published widely on the development of alcohol and drug laws. Professor Solomon has served as a consultant to Health and Welfare Canada, the Law Reform Commission of

Canada, and Toronto's Addiction Research Foundation.

**Patricia Erickson** is a Senior Scientist at the Centre for Addiction and Mental Health and adjunct professor of criminology at the University of Toronto. She has published extensively in the area of illicit drugs and drug policy, and is the author of the pioneering study, Cannabis Criminals: The Social Effects of Punishment on Drug Users (1980).

**Diane Riley** is a former Senior Policy Analyst with the Canadian Centre on Substance Abuse, and a director of the International Harm Reduction Association. Dr. Riley has authored many papers on cannabis, drug policy, and harm reduction.

**Marc Emery** is a well-known Vancouver activist and publisher of Cannabis Culture magazine. Emery also founded Hemp B.C. retail and seed sales, offering mail order delivery of hundreds of marijuana varieties via the Internet, *The Cannabis Café* (North America's first cannabis restaurant and "smoke room"), and the BC Marijuana Party.

**Bruce Alexander** is a retired Professor of Psychology at Simon Fraser University. Professor Alexander has been interested in drug issues and policy since 1970, undertaking research in the areas of addiction therapy and drug use among university students. He is the author of Peaceful Measures: Canada's Way Out of the "War on Drugs" (1990), a book relating psychological theory to Canadian drug policy.

**Gil Puder** is a decorated veteran of the Vancouver Police Department. Puder was an outspoken critic of Canadian drug control policy and law enforcement who, often acting in defiance of his superiors, aired his views in media and other public forums. Before his untimely death from cancer, Puder authored Crossfire: A Street Cop's Stand Against Violence, Corruption and the War on Drugs (1999).

**Neil Boyd** is Director of the Criminology Research Centre at Simon Fraser University. Professor Boyd has written extensively on drug control policy and substance criminalization and is the author of High Society: Legal and Illegal Drugs in Canada (1991).

**Jan Skirrow** is the former Chief Executive Officer of the Canadian Centre on Substance Abuse and the Alberta Alcohol and Drug Abuse Commission, and a former Deputy Minister of Community and Occupational Health for the province of Alberta. Working in the field of addictions since the 1960's, he was involved provincially, nationally, and internationally in the development and promotion of the harm reduction model.

**Chris Clay** is former proprietor of the Hemp Nation retail store in London, Ontario. His constitutional challenge of Canada's cannabis laws—following the 1995-1996 police raids on his store from which he was charged with possession, cultivation, and trafficking of marijuana, and faced the possibility of a life sentence in prison—brought together expert witnesses from addictions and drug studies (some of whom were interviewed in the present study) and provides important insight into legal and political obstacles to drug reform in Canada. Mr. Clay was found guilty of trafficking and cultivating a narcotic and sentenced to three years probation

.

**Eugene Oscapella** is an Ottawa lawyer and founding member of the Canadian Foundation for Drug Policy. He currently maintains the CFDP Website, a comprehensive database for disseminating research and independent views on drug policy issues, and has frequently appeared before Parliamentary committees and public hearings, and presented at conferences on Canadian drug policy.

The fact that the participants are identifiable public figures made the sampling procedure and preparation for interviewing quite different than in many other studies (Spector 1980). The interviewing was conducted at a later stage, being used to supplement the data I had gathered previously from documentary sources. Because I was able to ask specific questions raised in the course of documentary research, the interviews were not entirely exploratory; but they were unstructured, allowing me to seek interpretations that are often missing from official public documents. This excerpt from my interview with Dr. Diane Riley, a co-founder of the International Harm Reduction Association, illustrates the value of such first-hand information. Prior to the interview, I had accumulated a great deal of documentary material on the harm reduction movement. These had created the impression that harm reduction was becoming the dominant perspective of drug policy participants. Having learned of an upcoming meeting of the UN to address global drug issues, I was eager to discuss this with an expert in the area. However, I discovered how limited my knowledge was about the progress of the harm reduction movement.

When asked about the meeting, Dr. Riley stated: "That's at the beginning of June in New York and a number of groups have made application to attend, including the International Association. We haven't heard back; I imagine we're not going to be asked. I mean we were more or less told with a name like Harm Reduction Association, they're not going to ask us... [Why wouldn't a harm reduction group like yours be granted official standing at this meeting?] Because of the name; the UN is very opposed to harm reduction... [I had assumed this was a widely accepted paradigm today?] Oh no, absolutely not! No, the accepted paradigm by the UN is prohibition. And there is no funding whatsoever; they will not fund countries that do harm reduction.... No, it's quite the opposite." The excerpt illustrates that studying public figures involves extensive preparation and ongoing exploration. Advance knowledge about informants' work, and other information that is in the public record, is also important for establishing rapport.

Spector (1980, p. 100-101) notes that well-known people tend to expect this work: "They may grow impatient with questions that could easily be answered by a look at public documents or their writings, or they may not take an uninformed researcher seriously." The interviewer must be aware of the critical issues and pursue them directly when necessary. Ideally, however, as rapport becomes established and the interview progresses, the questioning becomes more open-ended or unstructured so as to generate unique insights and the sharing of information. As experienced claims makers, who actively have sought to articulate their views about Canadian drug policy, one would expect that public figures are willing research participants; and the expectation was met in this study. While practical concerns like geographical proximity and timing put some limits on our ability to meet, other ways of making contact such telephone and email, also were available and used if necessary. Informants were contacted via email in most cases and a private meeting was requested. Only one of fourteen public figures I contacted did not reply to my written request; and all who responded agreed to be interviewed.

Most interviews took place in the greater Toronto area, and five of them were done in the city of Vancouver. All but two of them were done in person (one was interviewed by phone and the other via email); and of eleven done in person, seven of them were recorded. In the others, tape recording was deemed overly conspicuous or inappropriate for the setting, such as in a noisy restaurant or bar. On those occasions with

33

disruptions and/or privacy concerns, the majority of note taking was done after the interview. While constructing notes from memory may sacrifice the detail needed for the use of direct quotes, talk in casual settings uninhibited by microphones provide an opportunity to evoke greater candour and information sharing by informants. Two memorable examples come from separate discussions (one in Vancouver and another six months later in Toronto) that I had with Constable Gil Puder. Having gained wide recognition for his candid opposition to punitive drug control policies, at the time of our first meeting Puder was put under a "gag order" by the Vancouver Chief of Police.

Despite his willingness to go 'on the record' against orders, the possibility that Puder might face disciplinary action was a nonetheless salient issue. Our more casual discussions better suit the circumstances; and I learned a great deal about the politics of policing that may not have been forthcoming under interview conditions. Although documentary research and unstructured interviewing were the primary methods for collection of the data, informal interactions with participants—including 'participant observation' as opposed to interviewing at a 1998 drug conference in Toronto—are among the many data sources in this study. As a conference participant, I had the opportunity to interact informally with experts I had interviewed and reestablish contact in a more casual setting. I was introduced to other well known people in the process who I may not have met otherwise. Research involving public figures as an ethnographic process can produce such a quantity of rich, varied data that the problem arises of how to analyze them and present study conclusions so as to convince others of their validity.

The present work involves the in-depth study of a small sample of informants selected to represent a specific organization or drug policy perspective. From the evidence gathered a more general set of concepts are to be inferred from particular persons and the social processes under investigation. Such analytical procedures are difficult to summarize and rarely presented adequately, with the full weight of evidence for conclusions and the processes by which they were reached, for the reader to assess. However, despite the objections of scientists adhering to more 'rigorous' methodologies, often such disputes about field research reliability rest on the unwarranted assumption that researchers should set out to answer all the same questions. According to Becker (1970, p. 40-41): "People often study the same or similar organizations using field methods but have different theories and different questions in mind. When they ask different questions, they get different answers...but the difference does not indicate that the information is untrustworthy. It shows only that the observer is observing something different."

Concerning the validity of field research evidence, Becker argues the lack of strict rules in field work is more of a strength than a weakness. Since the field researcher is not constrained by detailed and inflexible procedural rules, he or she can use different ways of getting at the questions of interest and a variety of devices to elicit talk by informants. Countering the argument that such unstructured methods serve only to accentuate the bias of researchers, Becker (1970, p. 56) states, "...the more different kinds of observations one makes, the more difficult it becomes to ignore or explain away evidence that runs counter to one's expectation or bias." Where field work methods are appropriate, the more active role of the researcher—using numerous items of information and flexible procedures—allows us to test our conclusions repeatedly and in a variety of ways. And although the use of flexible procedures in field work may make comparability complicated to achieve, it also facilitates development of innovative strategies to elicit further information. Producing "fuller data" through triangulated methods (Denzin 1970) warrants greater confidence in field research conclusions.

Because the field researcher draws on many different types of statements and items of data in support of his or her conclusions, Becker dismisses concerns about validity. With Rose (1945), he argues that the use of the standardized survey or schedule is only appropriate in research seeking data on the prevalence of a certain attitude in a defined population. Where fuller information as to the nature of a given attitude is needed, a more active role on the part of the researcher is highly desirable. According to Becker, for example, researchers often inhibit themselves by adopting an overly accommodating interview style designed to establish an easy rapport or to avoid 'leading' the respondent. Such a non-reflexive approach to interviewing fails to take advantage of the researcher's presence in the situation, further negating the production of evidence based on our own experiences and the ways people respond to us as observers. If, as is the case here, we actually engage in the same style of life and activities as the people we study, we can make use of our own responses to the tasks and troubles of the situation.[*]

Through the use of strategic conversational tactics, even taking up positions ourselves on some of the issues, the creative interviewer can elicit more candid statements than would be normally forthcoming. Becker (1970) discusses a number of tactics, such as the use of skepticism or "playing dumb" about implied understandings, with the aim to elicit more candid from respondents than they had originally intended. Insofar as my informants were deliberately selected for their public statements in the cannabis debate, their

---

[*] These ideas are developed in additional detail in Hathaway, A.D. and Atkinson, M.F. 2003. Active Interview Tactics in Research on Public Deviants: Exploring the Two-Cop Personas. Field Methods 15(2): 161-185.

truthfulness *per se* was not in question. However, Becker's tactical approach to interviewing, with its call for flexible responses on the part of the researcher, did not go unheeded in the conduct of this study. Notwithstanding the importance of preparing for the interviews, sometimes playing dumb, or putting questions to informants at the risk of sounding uninformed, is a useful strategy for seeking information or confirmation on assumptions that otherwise may not be so forthcoming. The following example centres on the understanding about the 'US influence' on Canadian drug policy.

After noting several factors that might spur drug law reform, Professor Alan Young addressed the major obstacles to change: "...what is opposing is the big mystery. That's something I can only speculate upon.... Considering the fact that most of western Europe has moved in the direction of law reform and most of Australia has, I'm left with the conclusion that the only reason why Canada is not moved by this issue is our geographical proximity to the United States, which for their own bizarre and perverse reasons believe that the war on drugs is an important part of their domestic policy. And they have no trouble dismissing developments in the Netherlands and Germany and Spain... [So Canada and the US are very much linked in respect to drug policy?] Of course they are! What, you don't think the United States doesn't flex their muscle around the world on their drug policy?... They have troops in Bolivia. They have troops in Columbia. They've tried to cut deals with Burma and other Southeast Asian countries in the Golden Triangle. They use the drug war as an excuse to infiltrate other countries and influence their national policy. So there's no question in my mind that they're the primary drug warriors in the world, and I can't think of another country that takes the same stance."

By playing dumb about the subject, my question prompted the informant to explicate more vividly a point that had heretofore been implicit. Whereas such tactics should not be used indiscriminately, nor will they prove effective in all situations, there are certain benefits to taking a more flexible and reflexive approach to the data. Although difficult to summarize and present with the full weight of evidence collected for the reader to assess, in the following discussion I have nonetheless endeavoured to construct a "natural history" (Becker 1958) of the research process. The problem of presenting 'proof' of findings or conclusions is addressed below in terms of influential choices made in my analysis of drug reform claims making.

**Problems of Inference and Proof in a Study of Public Figures**
Becker (1958) notes that whereas participant observations and similar techniques may be gathered in

standardized form capable of being transformed into legitimate statistical data, the contingencies of the field usually prevent the collection of data in such a form as to meet the assumptions of statistical tests. The kinds of evidence gathered may vary considerably, as will the observer's confidence in his or her conclusions. But when it comes to assessing the evidence for conclusions, the qualitative researcher takes a cue from his statistical colleagues. According to Becker (1958, p. 656, italics in original): "Instead of arguing that a conclusion is either totally true or false, he decides, if possible, how *likely* it is that his conclusion about the frequency or distribution of some phenomenon is an accurate quasi-statistic, just as the statistician decides, on the basis of the varying values of a correlation coefficient or a significance figure, that his conclusion is more or less likely to be accurate."

When carried out in the field these operations are not conducted as systematically as they might be and the overall assessment is ordinarily postponed until the final stages of data analysis, in which the individual findings are incorporated into a generalized descriptive model which best explains the data. Conclusions at this stage, Becker notes, consist of statements about necessary and sufficient conditions for the existence of some phenomenon, statements that some phenomenon exercises a persistent and continuing influence on diverse events, or statements identifying a situation as an instance of some phenomenon described more abstractly in sociological theory. Despite efforts to formalize this operation (e.g., through factor and relational analysis of survey data), qualitative research is still needed insofar as statistics are inadequate to express their conceptions for which the use of words is necessary.

Through the sequential process of analytic induction (Lindesmith 1947), the observer begins by constructing a model to specify interrelations among variables. Greater accuracy is sought by successively refining the model to account for negative cases that do not square well with prior formulations. The researcher may have the problem well conceptualized and be able to infer what kinds of evidence are likely to support or refute a provisional model, and thereby formulate hypotheses in a deliberate search for negative instances, or he or she may as yet be unaware of the problem. The best evidence, for Becker (1958, p. 659): "…may be that gathered in the most unthinking fashion, when the observer has simply recorded the item although it has no place in the system of concepts and hypotheses he is working with at the time, for there might be less bias produced by the wish to substantiate or repudiate a particular idea." Evidence gathered actively and deliberately for testing hypotheses may carry greater weight for certain kinds of conclusions, but the researcher is more convinced of a conclusion's validity when there are many kinds of evidence to support it.

Qualitative data frequently consists of many different kinds of observations that cannot be counted and categorized without losing some of their value as evidence. Unlike statistical data, which can be neatly summarized in tables and the methods are systematized for reporting in shorthand fashion, most qualitative data and analytical procedures do not lend themselves to such ready summary. Seldom are they overviewed in sufficient length for the reader to follow the details of the analysis and assess on what basis the conclusions have been reached. As a possible solution to presenting proof of findings, Becker (1958, p. 660) argues for a "natural history" of conclusions, "...presenting the evidence as it came to the attention of the observer during the successive stages of his conceptualization of the problem...so that the reader is given greater access to the data and procedures on which conclusions are based." A natural history of findings from the present study follows. Clearly it is not feasible to present all the evidence, nor every datum put to use in conceptualizing the problem. My aim is to address key analytical procedures and inferences, to allow the reader to assess the adequacy of proof and degree of confidence that can be assigned to the conclusions.

**Sampling and Interviewing Procedures:** The interviews commenced after analysis of documents to identify participants and prevalent claims making in the Canadian context of drug policy debate. Data were gathered from a wide range of materials including academic publications, transcripts of court and parliamentary proceedings, video tapes, television news and press reports, editorial columns and print media, drug reform newsgroups and Websites, pamphlets, newsletters, and other activist literature. After several months of documentary research to identify the 'key players' in the cannabis debate, I had compiled a list of several dozen potential respondents, including politicians and government officials, academic analysts and other professionals working in drug policy organizations, representatives of the legal profession and different branches of law enforcement, and well-known activists and defendants from past and present legal challenges.

From the original list of names gleaned from documentary data, I began contacting for interviews the better known public figures, those mentioned repeatedly in the literature and media coverage of the issue and thus associated with common claims or counter-claims. Once each was contacted and agreed to meet, I started a more intensive search for materials written by and about him or her in preparation for our interview. In this way, I was able to formulate an unstructured guide for each interview, comprising specific questions and broader topics for discussion. Though the interview guides were designed to address important issues and contentions found within the documents, typically they were employed only as a back-up for stimulating conversation or probing for more information. Encouraging informants to work from their own definitions of the problem, interviews were prefaced by my request for their consent "...to participate in an interview about Canadian marijuana policy that is intended to facilitate the sharing of information...towards a better understanding of how legislation becomes practiced and possibly even changed in this country."

Compared to direct questioning, which can prompt answers that may have not otherwise occurred to informants, the volunteered statement carries greater evidential weight, for it is less likely to reflect the preoccupations and possible biases of the researcher (Becker 1958). Thus, despite the need to be prepared for interviewing, the interviews were nonetheless largely exploratory. The participants were encouraged to take the lead in our discussions with only occasional prompting and probing on my part. As experienced claims makers well accustomed to being in the public eye, my informants were not only articulate speakers evidently at ease during interview situations—it soon became clear that they expected to be quoted and would hold me responsible for quoting them directly. Indeed, notes Spector (1980, p. 106), speaking on the record can be an important motivation for informants to participate in such research where "...statements derive their significance from the fact that they are said by public figures whose previous statements are a matter of record."

Public figures ordinarily assume they will be named and identified with their statements. Accordingly, unlike in surveys sampling from very large populations where the names of individuals or organizations play no role in the analysis, the standard guarantees of anonymity and confidentiality ordinarily extended to research participants may be unnecessary and technically undesirable (Rainwater and Pittman 1967). Standard ethical commitments in this study, like assuring the participants that they could withdraw from the interview at any time or refuse to answer certain questions, were emphasized in writing when obtaining their consent. Participants were also informed before signing that in the final reports of the study they "may be identified by name and/or organizational affiliation" and that "unless otherwise specified the interview will be audiotaped." The request was readily agreed to by all those I interviewed in person, and only two respondents indicated they may wish to "stop the tape" when answering certain questions (though this request was never made by any interviewee).

As a gesture of my commitment to fair and accurate reporting, I informed the participants that at the conclusion of the project a copy of the finished report would be made available to them on request. Although only a few of them expressed any interest in receiving the final report—an observation shared by Spector in his research on public figures—the gesture seemed important as a way of establishing trust and a rapport conducive to the open sharing of information. When research participants are identified in the analysis and have full access to the finished report, the researcher is held accountable to informants and other researchers alike. As noted by Spector (1980, p. 106): "Identifying sources also provides a check on the researcher, because sources can then deny the statement or attempt to disassociate themselves from it. It also makes possible replication by other scholars in a way that is not possible if identities are concealed. The practice of granting anonymity, said to protect the research subject, also shields the researcher from criticism and refutation both by the informants and by other scholars."

Although none of my informants were concerned about being identified, nor did they seem particularly interested in my findings, knowing that the final report would be available may have contributed to building a more open sense of trust. For some of my informants, it seemed perfectly natural to take part in a predominantly one-sided conversation for hours at a time with little prompting on my part (interviews ranged between 30 minutes and four hours in duration, depending on the receptivity and time constraints of the informant). Others took a more passive approach to the interview, treating me perhaps just as they would a journalist, which required me asking direct questions and more probing. My informants seemed to appreciate the extent of my preparation for interviews and the special interest I had taken in their views and activities. Many of them provided me with additional documentary materials and contacts I may not have obtained otherwise, and extended the invitation to keep in touch should further questions arise.

After each interview, informants were asked to suggest other informants to broaden the sample. Some asked me directly who else I would be speaking to, at which point I informed them who I had interviewed and asked them to suggest others. In this way I hoped to expand my list of potential interviewees, taking special note of names mentioned repeatedly, and verify the importance to the study of informants already included in the sample. When studying public figures, this means of sample verification is a particular advantage of the 'snowball sampling' strategy. The naming of potential respondents by others in this study reinforced those already identified in the analysis of documents beforehand. One exception is Jan Skirrow, a former Director of several drug policy organizations now living in retirement on Canada's west coast. It might be argued that withdrawing from the policy arena should exclude him from a study with emphasis on public figures. But former public figures who have stepped back from the spotlight can offer insights from a standpoint unhindered by such pressures; and they should not be ruled out as participants.

More generally, corroborating Spector's (1980) observations, my informants were not only happy to participate—like many other research participants, they were evidently flattered I considered their activities so worthy of attention. Many of my informants were social scientists themselves. We shared a common language of reference and rapport often developed naturally in the course of conversation. I was often asked during interviews where I stood on the issues in question, and I made no attempt to hide my opinions. At the same time, following Spector (1980, p. 103), I made clear that understanding the broader "process and dynamics of controversy" was the primary objective of my research. I stated my intention to interview people on all sides of the controversy, asking respondents to name informants with opposing perspectives on the cannabis issue. In this way I hoped to expand my list of contacts to allow for equal representation of status quo defenders and reformers alike. During the course of documentary research, however, it soon became evident that the former would be harder to come by.

Although our legal institutions and various branches of drug law enforcement have spokespeople who are responsible for making public statements, these are made sporadically and in an official capacity only, reflecting institutional arrangements that cannot be identified with any particular individual. Institutionalized support for the status quo seems largely interchangeable from one public official to the next, for it is the office or position rather than its occupant that is generally considered to be public. To support this contention, it is noteworthy that despite attempts to identify status quo supporters through a follow-up of names gleaned from media sources, none were found to meet the criteria for inclusion in the study. Put otherwise, the names of officials representing our legal institutions were encountered only sporadically and seldom repeatedly in the course of documentary research. Whereas the relevant spokespeople may be identified through channels that are made available to the general public, officials operating in a public relations capacity are not afforded the same status as public figures in this study.

**Delimiting the Sample and Conceptual Focus:** My original intention was to interview informants on 'both sides' of the cannabis issue. The decision to shift focus was considered in the stages of documentary research after failing to identify a comparable contingent of public figures seeking to defend the status quo. After interviewing started, this unanticipated turn was reinforced at times 'off tape' by assertions like the following: "You'll have a hard time finding anyone who will stand up for prohibition." Likewise, activist Chris Clay, citing strong support for marijuana law reform, said "It's hard to find anyone who can justify the current prohibition. Even the government's only witness in my trial, Dr. Harold Kalant, called for decriminalization." Two noteworthy exceptions I encountered in the study were both Ontario lobby groups who insisted on maintaining criminal penalties for cannabis for the 'sake of our children.' At a 1996 hearing on proposed changes to the law (Standing Senate Committee on Legal and Constitutional Affairs: Ottawa, April 24), Charles Perkins, the Chairman of Lambton's "Families in Action" and Fred Burford, former President of Toronto's Council on Drug Abuse, vociferously argued against the proposition.

I encountered Fred Burford in person two years later at a Toronto drug policy conference, where he stood as the lone advocate for prohibition in a room of drug reform supporters. The central claims for prohibition must be countered by reformers, who shape their arguments accordingly, and at points in the analysis will need to be addressed. But while the lack of activism in support of prohibition did exert an influence on sampling decisions, the more cohesive character of anti-drug discourses suggests a theoretical motivation also for delimiting the sample as I did. Because our longstanding legal institutions rest on the authority of "presumption" (Czubaroff 1989), the onus or burden of proof is placed on reformers to warrant changes in policy. Documentary analysis of official statements and testimony presented at legislative hearings supports the contention that prohibitionist claims, unlike the more highly differentiated arguments of cannabis reform advocates, are based on a uniform set of assumptions that fit the description of "endangerment rhetoric."

Endangerment themes inciting public fear and outrage over the immorality of drug use, though couched in more scientific terminology today, are largely unchanged since the early days of prohibition. The resilience and longevity of these claims, despite the wealth of evidence to the contrary, underscores the efficiency of arguments invoking 'social values' and obstacles facing those who seek to supplant them. Public statements by pro-prohibition lobby groups, for example, are consistent in their use of endangerment rhetoric which will be illustrated in some detail later on. Such claims are often questionable in the light of research evidence; however, their accuracy, or factual basis, is of little relevance here. Public fears (particularly parents') are responsive to endangerment themes that invest certain drugs with the insidious power to enslave our young people. As noted earlier, the power of these statements may be somewhat weaker in the context of more 'rational' debate. More importantly perhaps, they are delivered nonetheless with the full authority of moral-legal presumption needed to uphold drug prohibition.

While the rational discourse of science is used often by drug policy reformers and prohibitionists alike, only the latter are able to lay claim to moral warrants that are taken for granted. Despite evident support for law reform among Canadians, the criminal status of cannabis is still widely assumed. Prohibitionist claim making in the media and parliament, and other public forums for debates about the law, have adhered to standard scripts or talking points in which endangerment themes are invoked. Anti-prohibition claims, by contrast, have not only garnered more attention from the public, but also are becoming more complex and diversified as well. Below, the conceptual focus on rhetoric is developed in terms of its natural history, based on my recollections and note taking in this study of Canadian drug reform advocates.

**Conceptually Developing the Focus on Rhetoric:** On delimiting my sample to drug policy reformers, analysis proceeded by way of theoretical sampling (Glaser and Strauss 1967) aimed at seeking out negative instances of the emerging concepts. Inferences and conclusions emerging in the course of documentary analysis were processually refined during interviews wherein I sought to test my guiding assumptions through analytic induction and the constant comparative method. The juxtaposition of primary themes, described previously as endangerment and entitlement rhetoric, as a general distinction is supported by the data. Although the former is rhetorically consistent across cases, the noted differentiation of entitlement discourses required a more intense investigation. The focus of this research on claims making that emerges is surrounding the distinction between a morally invested, human rights perspective and the harm reduction movement's value neutral stance on drugs.

Over the later stages of fieldwork and analysis, the emphasis on drug reform rhetoric emerged as a conceptual refinement of my focus on claims making. Thus my understanding of the research problem shifted from exploring claims on different sides of the debate into an ethnographic investigation and analysis of the nuances of drug reform discourse. Studies centring on rhetorical work as the avowed axis for data collection and analysis are rare in any discipline. Exploring social problems from a constructionist perspective provides the theoretical and analytical tools needed to rigorously investigate rhetorical styles and strategies within a well established sociological framework. Building on the literature reviewed in the first chapter, the differentiated character of drug reform discourses is a compelling illustration of the complexity of claims makers' demands and their audiences, which was noted in earlier research by Best (1987).

In the chapters that follow, harm reduction is developed in terms of its assumptions and rhetorical limitations with specific reference to the cannabis debate. Another focus of discussion is the human rights perspective. I will argue there are benefits to actively engaging the rhetorical strengths of the liberal tradition, such as upholding norms of tolerance and respect for freedom over morally objectionable government intrusions into the private lives of its citizens. The liberal ideology shared by my informants, despite the tendency of most to seek distance from the label by adopting scientific standards and styles of rational argumentation, reinforced my emphasis on discursive strategies. Collins dictionary defines stratagem or strategy as an overall plan, or trick—an art of war. Hence, by definition, a strategy suggests a certain amount of duplicity or artifice is involved. This is an observation that has certain implications for the role of social science in public policy arenas. The noted tension between scientific objectivity and advocacy that so evidently frustrated a number of my informants is taken up in further detail later in this book.

## Summary

Studying public figures makes use of sampling and interviewing procedures that are quite different from most other field studies. Some of the challenges are unique to research on public figures—requiring, in addition to attention to some problems also found in other types of field work, the use of innovative strategies to address these issues. This chapter emphasizes the respective contributions of Howard Becker and Malcolm Spector to the conduct of empirically defensible field work and to researching public figures as social problems participants. Becker's (1958) "natural history" approach to presentation of evidence from field research was employed with reference to sampling and interviewing procedures and the conceptual emergence of the present study focus.

Further, I acknowledge Woolgar and Pawluch's (1985) contribution in critiquing what they saw as unavoidable inconsistencies in the selective relativism of social problems explanations. The authors characterize their aim as an attempt to work toward an "ethnography of argument." They portray the work of scientific explanation as a practical accomplishment, emphasizing "...the advantages of not taking for granted those activities of argument in which we ourselves participate" (p. 214n). In this vein, turning to address the data gathered in this study of Canadian claims making for drug policy reform, the predominant rhetorical perspectives are examined towards a better understanding of discursive characteristics, and strategic benefits as well as limitations.

## CHAPTER THREE
## HARM REDUCTION STRATEGIES FOR CANNABIS

In this chapter, harm reduction is examined with an eye to differentiate its founding principles from ways the term is commonly misused. It is observed that harm reduction is increasingly co-opted by groups with little tolerance for substance use and having the ultimate objective of no use of drugs at all. I will examine some proposals to reduce the harm of drug laws, and to promote safer consumption of cannabis. Proposed decriminalization models are also are looked at before turning to the limitations of the harm reduction movement, with specific reference to marijuana law reform.

### Defining Harm Reduction

Developing from about 1990 on in the drug field, the harm reduction perspective stems from the response by public health agencies to the emergence of AIDS in the 1980's, and the idea that providing clean needles to intravenous drug users saves lives. Public fears over the spread of AIDS among drug users, and from drug users into the general population, endorsed widespread understanding of the epidemic as posing a greater threat to health than the dangers of drug use itself. Preeminently pragmatic in its approach to the problem of drug abuse, harm reduction recognizes illicit drug use as an inescapable fact, rather than a moral issue, and seeks to reduce the individual and social costs of drug *abuse*, rather than eliminating all drug use *per se*. Emphasizing scientific standards of rationality, harm reduction avoids issuing moral challenges to prohibition in favour of cost-benefit analyses addressing specific problem behaviours in pragmatic rather than ideological terms (Erickson 1997a). Its growth and diffusion among health professionals and analysts in the multidisciplinary field of drug studies has so broadened the original meaning of the concept that other terms, such as harm minimization, risk reduction, and risk minimization are sometimes used interchangeably.

**Harm Versus Risk:** Despite use of these terms as if they were synonymous, definitional conventions have rhetorical significance that warrant further discussion. Attempting to clarify use of such

45

terms as *harm* versus *risk*, and its qualifier *reduction* versus *minimization*, helps delineate rhetorical features of these terms, suggesting a somewhat narrower definition of harm reduction. Although the term risk reduction is often used as if it were synonymous with harm reduction, it is important to emphasize that risk behaviour does not necessarily result in harm. Unlike other, often more dangerous, forms of risk taking—such as car racing, mountain climbing, boxing and bungee jumping—which are tolerated and even encouraged by society, drug taking has been singled out as something inherently evil. Accordingly, because it operates in the grey areas between extremes, accepting the possibility of drug taking under certain circumstances, harm reduction has not been easily defined or promoted, and is often seen as promoting intolerable behaviour (Riley 1996).

Despite its ideological limitations one might argue that *harm reduction* surely is the best guide to policy. For whereas harm may be taken as the event itself or as relating to the event, the concept of risk relates to the possibility that the event might occur, and is thereby only a surrogate for the harm that is, or is likely to be, incurred. According to Strang (1993, p. 5), for example: "Harm must surely be our target. Support for competing proposals should be determined by the extent to which they reduce or increase the amount of harm accrued by the individual, the community or society.... There may be times when we choose to look at ways of reducing risk, but this would only be because we felt that this was a more useful 'handle' on the possible harm which may be incurred." In a recent study of "risk reduction" among groups that promote marijuana and psychedelic drugs it was found that the kinds of risk reduction advocated go beyond the usual definitions of drug risk.

More specifically, notes Jenks (1995, p. 634): "Not only do these groups attempt to reduce the physical and psychological risks associated with using these drugs, but they are also concerned with reducing what are seen as greater risks associated with (1) draconian laws against drugs (including property forfeiture laws and mandatory minimum sentences), (2) overzealous law enforcement practices and drug testing, (3) sensationalistic government and media campaigns against drugs, and (4) mainstream views about drugs and users based on misinformation and prejudice." Whereas these issues may be interpreted in terms of risk, with focus on reducing the possibility that some foreseeable harm may occur, they more directly concern the actual harms being inflicted by overly punitive drug laws and the misinformation that shapes mainstream beliefs about illegal drugs and drug users.

To illustrate, NORML's (1993, p. 10) statement on the "ethical responsibilities of marijuana use" asks users to first "Do No Harm," so as not to jeopardize the safety of property or people, and to "Know What You Are Doing"—to learn about the physical and psychological effects of marijuana, and differentiate between use and abuse in their own consumption before attempting to persuade others that marijuana can be used responsibly by the general public. Marijuana users are further asked to "Help Others," to identify

46

themselves as members of a persecuted group and help the approximately 300,000 people arrested in the United States each year for marijuana offenses, and to "Help Change The Laws," by showing that marijuana users are responsible citizens and getting involved in the political process to repeal marijuana laws.

As noted by Jenks (1995, p. 634): "This broadening of the customary notions of risk reduction can be seen to expand greatly Becker's (1967) seminal hypothesis that a crucial function of drug subcultures is to educate drug users about the hazardous effects of drug use." More to the point of the present discussion, politically active "drug subcultures," like their professional counterparts pressing for drug law reform, ultimately seek to reduce drug related harm rather than risk, and so their claims tend most often to be stated specifically in terms of harm.

**Harm Reduction Strategies and the Goal of Harm Minimization:** Taken broadly, as bestowed with a multitude of meanings, harm reduction is generally agreeable, in principle at least, to liberal reformers and prohibitionists alike. As a general goal, the reduction of drug-related harm seems a rather trivial assumption with nothing much to offer as a practical guide to policy. This point was made as well in a report by the Canadian Centre on Substance Abuse (CCSA). It argues: "As a general goal, all drug policies and programs aim to reduce the harm associated with drug use. As a general goal, harm reduction is a very broad term. Virtually all drug policies and programs—including criminalization of users and abstinence oriented programs—have a goal of harm reduction" (Single et al. 1995). Funded largely from Canada's newly minted Drug Strategy, the CCSA was created by an Act of Parliament in 1988 to serve as a national focus for drug and alcohol issues. With the expiration of the Strategy and drastic reduction of funding in 1997, the Centre's active role as independent government think-tank on issues pertaining to policy was dramatically reduced to the function of a "clearinghouse" for disseminating information and maintaining a variety of databases on drug abuse.

As a past Chairman of the CCSA National Working Group on addictions policy and marijuana epidemiologist at the Addiction Research Foundation (ARF), Eric Single is well-versed in problems of definition and implementing harm reduction strategies for cannabis. Single emphasizes the importance of distinguishing between harm reduction as a goal and harm reduction as a strategy. Whereas all drug policies and programs aim to reduce drug-related harm, not all policies and programs with a goal of harm reduction employ harm reduction strategies. As a specific strategy, harm reduction takes on a narrower definition, referring only to policies and programs aimed at reducing drug-related harm without requiring abstention from drug use. Strang (1993, p. 7) likewise defines harm reduction in essentially operational terms, as a strategy rather than a goal, suggesting the term "harm minimisation" might refer to the overall goal or end point to be achieved by means of harm reduction; "...thus a harm-minimisation policy or approach might reasonably comprise various harm-reduction elements." The term harm reduction is accordingly reserved

47

for strategies prioritizing the proactive engagement of individuals, target groups, and communities to reduce the negative consequences of drug use while the user continues to use drugs, at least for the present time.

Whereas a harm reduction approach to personal drug use in the short term does not rule out longer term abstinence, it is generally understood that "...if a person is not willing to give up his or her drug use, we should assist them in reducing harm to himself or herself and others" (Buning 1993). The key aspects of this conceptualization, argues Single (1997), are that the user's decision to use drugs is accepted as fact, and the user is treated with dignity as a normal human being. Concerning longer term goals of intervention, harm reduction is neutral. No moral judgment is made either for or against drug use, regardless of the level or mode of consumption. The dignity and rights of the drug user are respected. In return, it is expected that he or she will behave responsibly, or "normally," as a citizen with rights and obligations under the law. Furthermore, it is acknowledged that, while carrying risks, drug use is a common feature of human experience that can also provide the user with benefits that must be taken into account if drug using behaviour is to be properly understood (Single et al. 1995).

The problem of balancing costs and benefits, and subsequent difficulties gathering the support needed to implement harm reduction policies, is to be examined at greater length in chapter four. For present purposes I emphasize, as a matter of definition, that in practice harm reduction's primary focus is on drug related harm as opposed to drug use in itself. As stated by Single and colleagues: "The fact or extent of a person's drug use per se is of secondary importance to the risk of harms consequent to use. The harms addressed can be related to health, social, economic or a multitude of other factors, affecting the individual, the community and society as a whole. Therefore, the first priority is to decrease the negative consequences of drug use to the user and to others, as opposed to focusing on decreasing the drug use itself. Harm reduction neither excludes nor presumes the long-term treatment goal of abstinence. In some cases, reduction of level of use may be one of the most effective forms of harm reduction. In others, alteration to the mode of use may be more effective" (Single et al. 1995).

Accordingly, notes Single (1997), the preferred definition of harm reduction is limited to strategies aimed at continued users. Thus conceived, abstinence oriented programs and the use of criminal law to deter drug use are not harm reduction measures. Despite compelling arguments to oppose certain prohibitive policies, however, Single stresses the importance of neutrality regarding longer term goals of intervention and broader policy issues. To illustrate, he argues: "...although many harm-reduction proponents advocate drug policy reform and even legalization of illicit drugs, harm reduction should not and does not necessarily mean approval of drug use or support for legalization...drug policy reform and legalization would greatly facilitate harm reduction programming...but there are clearly ways of facilitating such programmes under current drug policy as well...harm reduction should be viewed as the middle ground where persons with

48

widely differing views on drug policy can agree with one another regarding practical, immediate ways to reduce drug-related harm among users (Single 1997, pp. 12-13).

Working within the existing framework of prohibition, insofar as harm reduction programs have been shown to have a positive impact on reducing the spread of HIV and other infections, and are now being expanded to include a broad variety of programming aimed at reducing the adverse consequences of both illegal and legal drug use, harm reduction has been a relatively successful movement. It has proven generally effective and gained increasing official acceptance in many countries. Moreover, for a time during the conduct of the study, harm reduction was officially recognized as the basis of Canada's Drug Strategy. As documented in a 1997 report by the Canadian Centre on Substance Abuse, launched in 1987, Canada's Drug Strategy involved a five year commitment of funds amounting to $210 million to combat drug abuse. Demand reduction programs, centring on prevention, education, treatment and rehabilitation, were officially emphasized over supply reduction in order to balance existing efforts to contain the supply of drugs on the street. At that time, the federal government had been spending approximately $168 million a year on both supply and demand reduction programs.

In 1992, Canada's Drug Strategy was renewed with additional funding, set at $270 million, and the explicit goal of harm reduction (CCSA 1997). Despite the official shift in focus from interdiction to harm reduction, the actual implementation of this goal has yet to be realized. In 1997 the Strategy was nominally discontinued, and recent legislation has suggested even further withdrawal from demand reduction programming. The Controlled Drugs and Substances Act (CDSA) provided police drug squads with additional resources for enforcing Canada's long standing policy of prohibition (Erickson 1997a). In light of contradictions between the official statements of Canada's Drug Strategy and its actual implementation, Erickson concluded that the shift from punitive approaches to a public health policy of harm reduction had not occurred, nor was it likely to unfold in the near future. The following discussion of harm reduction options for cannabis therefore reflects continuing political realities, addressing strategies consistent with continued criminalization prior to those that are contingent on marijuana law reform.

## Harm Reduction Options for Cannabis[*]

Compared to heroin, cocaine, and other addictive drugs that are generally agreed to be more harmful, cannabis is seldom prominently discussed in the context of harm reduction. Nevertheless, it is invariably the first drug proposed for reform during any discussion of drug policy—a discussion that often, even

---

[*] This section is developed in additional detail in Hathaway, A.D. and Erickson, P.G. 2003. Drug Reform Principles and Policy Debates: Harm Reduction Prospects for Cannabis in Canada. Journal of Drug Issues 33(3): 467-496.

49

unwittingly, involves harm reduction (Morgan, Riley, and Chesher 1993). Considering the criminal justice costs of enforcing the cannabis laws, and their ineffectiveness in deterring the activity, reformers have long argued that the harms inflicted by the threat and application of criminal sanctions far outweigh any actual harm associated with use of the drug. Indeed, notes Erickson (1997a, p. 6), although cannabis use is not without health risks: "Many commentators in the field who have serious and legitimate reservations about the impact of overall drug legalization or regulation on public health make an exception for cannabis...cumulative evidence about its low addictive property, relatively infrequent consumption by the large majority of users, and few adverse health and behavioural effects at low levels of use, have not seriously challenged the "soft" drug label bestowed in the late 1960's."

Due to some consensus on the lesser harms of cannabis as compared to so-called harder drugs, harm reduction options tend to emphasize reducing the adverse consequences of criminalization, rather than the practices of users of the drug. Based on rational assessments of the harms of either type, the harm reduction approach suggests that cannabis be normalized, treating users as members of society rather than outcasts (Erickson 1997a), to reduce at least the real harm of continued criminalization. Staunchly opposed to any loosening of restrictions on drug use, however, prohibitionists view the normalization of cannabis with great fear and actively promote its illegality (Morgan et al. 1993). Touting endangerment themes that are largely unchanged since the late 1970's, prohibitionists commonly argue that the cannabis today is of much higher potency or greater toxicity. Accordingly, it is claimed that cannabis use causes more clinical and biological harm and is much more dangerous than once thought. More importantly perhaps, cannabis consumption is claimed to be a "gateway," or "stepping stone," to the use of harder drugs.

Since cannabis use correlates with the use of more dangerous drugs like heroin and cocaine, the gateway hypothesis is a predominant claim in support of enforcing prohibition. Whereas it is generally conceded that cannabis is not as toxic as cocaine or heroin, evidence to support the stepping stone effect is widely cited in the literature (e.g., Nahas 1990; Kandel, Yamaguchi, and Chen 1992; Kandel and Yamaguchi 1993) and the notion of "Getting Tough on Gateway Drugs" (DuPont 1985) remains ever popular with anti-drug forces. Despite the enduring popularity and persuasiveness of the gateway argument, however, Morgan and his colleagues cast considerable doubt on the logic of its conclusions. As conceded by Kandel et al. (1992, p. 453), clearly there are temporal patterns in drug use, but "...the notion of stages in drug behavior does not imply that these stages are either obligatory or universal... ." Clearly, all psychoactive drug use tends to correlate with other psychoactive drug use, and most users of dangerous drugs have previously used less dangerous drugs, but so have they used many other kinds of substances for that matter, most notably those of the legal variety.

According to Morgan et al. (1993, p. 217): "Essentially all users of heroin have previously

50

consumed cannabis, alcohol, caffeine, nicotine and benzodiazepines.... Perhaps 60 million Americans have tried marijuana yet slightly more than two thirds have never tried another illegal drug. Cannabis seems more often to be a closed gate than a gateway in that its use signals the terminus of illegal drug experimentation." In a study done in Amsterdam, where cannabis use has been normalized and illicit drugs are readily available, it was found that although small numbers of experienced cannabis users do try other illicit substances, the use of cannabis tends to satisfy almost all curiosity (Cohen and Sas 1997). Despite growing evidence to reject the stepping stone hypothesis, its resilience as a mainstay of prohibitionist rhetoric reflects the symbolic power of criminal penalties. For gateway theory proponents, official acceptance of illicit drug use is unthinkable. Upholding prohibition is the only policy option, for attempting to normalize cannabis through harm reduction would only exacerbate the problem of drug abuse in our society or, worse yet, lead to the legalization of all drugs.

Recognizing the pervasiveness of fears concerning drug use and status quo arrangements opposing drug reform, as a matter of strategy, harm reductionists generally adopt rather moderate positions on policy. Whereas legislative change is often discussed as if it were inevitable, reform arguments from the harm reductionist perspective are non-adversarial in character, recognizing both the legitimacy of opposing concerns and potential problems attending policy implementation. In the following excerpts from my interview with Eric Single, he argues in favour of adopting a moderate standpoint on drug policy reform. He said: "It's never a good idea to take a stand on policy unless there is significant scientific evidence to back up that position. I consider myself fairly middle of the road on policy—I have a lot of liberal friends who don't think I go far enough. I've never been an advocate of outright legalization.... I think the solution for Canada is going to come from some of these middle, milder options, small incremental moves, not big moves to decriminalize or legalize things."

"It's not going to be a big sweep. It's going to come in gradual, small changes in response to the exigencies of the situation. They just can't afford to use up those kinds of resources on drugs. And there's a growing recognition in the law enforcement community that the long term solution is on the demand side and treatment.... I think that's the real wedge in the door to reform. It's not based on principles or ideals, or whatever particular bend you take in arguing for drug reform—that's not going to work.... I think the most valuable thing a researcher can do for drug reform is to do good, cost effective studies of harm reduction programs and things like that, and use that to argue to law enforcement that this is going to save you a lot of resources desperately needed in other areas.... I've always taken a liberal versus radical stance on these issues. I believe in working with the system in trying to convince people, rather than hoping the system gets so rotten that I see a reason for going 180 degrees in the opposite direction." [Is there cause to be optimistic in this regard?]

51

"Oh definitely. It's not for good reasons. It's not because people are becoming more enlightened. It's because the system just cannot afford to continue with its present policies much longer.... On one hand I am for reform on the basis of the economic cost of prohibitionist policy, but on the other hand there is a cautionary note for reform based on the harms of legal drug use. There is a reasonable fear.... The actual implementation of regulations is full of problems and conflict...and that's one of the major reasons why you shouldn't get into an adversarial position with the major players in the law enforcement community. Because whatever happens, they're going to have the final say on implementation.... The actual implementation of changes is just as important as the change in policy." As a former advisor to the Liquor License Board of Ontario, Single's account provides insight into matters of policy implementation that are often overlooked by drug policy reformers. He notes, for example, that public perceptions rather than research played the major role in determining the Advisory Committee's final recommendation to Cabinet.

Public perceptions had to be carefully gauged and weighted accordingly, and finally, in contrast to the original intent to liberalize the regulations and relax government control over public access to alcohol, they opted for a more cautious approach: "The operative policy was to find the middle ground that would keep the majority of people who have an opinion on the subject reasonably happy" (Single and Tocher 1992, p. 1441). Although it may not be surprising that research would play a minor role in policy deliberations, Single argues that researchers can do more to make their work relevant simply by tailoring analyses to address distinctive options. Considering the lack of research on the impact of policy options for a legal drug like alcohol, the lack of information available for cannabis is not altogether surprising. As with regulating alcohol, there are many issues that need to be addressed when considering changes to the marijuana laws. The problem of impaired driving is one such issue that requires further research, for example. Single told me: "I mean we don't have very good data on cannabis intoxication and driving. I don't think cannabis is totally benign for long term, chronic users but by and large it's no worse than alcohol. One of the things I'm worried about is people getting stoned and getting into cars. It's a potentially much greater problem than we realize at this point. Nobody's studying that that I'm aware of. I don't see any funding programs for marijuana, given the billions we're pouring into other things and other kinds of issues."

The issue of marijuana use and driving is examined in greater detail in the next chapter. For present purposes, the often argued call to follow through on shifting drug control priorities from supply to demand reduction, favours harm reduction measures over enforced abstinence, with emphasis instead on education and prevention. However, as with implementing alcohol reform, attempts to implement harm reduction oriented education programs have been fraught with difficulty. Here again, drug policy decisions are determined more by ideology than relevant research. Put otherwise, the practice of primary prevention, or 'demand reduction' through strict abstinence, remains the predominant paradigm in drug education. When it comes to protecting our children from drug use, the familiar "just say no" perspective, which is rooted in a prohibitionist tradition of law enforcement and augmented discursively by medical and religious paternalism, is generally considered the only publicly defensible approach to drug education. From a harm reduction standpoint, primary prevention does not work because it fails to recognize that drug use is normal, often beneficial, and only rarely leads to significant problems (Cohen 1993).

Harm reduction, notes Cohen, is secondary prevention—it considers benefits as well as risks in the context of where drug use actually takes place. In other words, *harm reduction is educational about rather than against drugs.* Harm reduction accepts drug use as a fact and suggests that when provided with accurate drug knowledge and treated as responsible citizens, drug users will behave responsibly and rationally. When properly informed and respected as a free individual, the drug user will seek to reduce potential harms to him or herself and others. Concerning cannabis and driving, for example, it is argued that, like drinkers, marijuana users may be accurately appraised of the dangers of driving under the influence. Thus informed, it is assumed that, as with alcohol, most users will respect legal standards of impairment and accept the consequences that may follow a detected violation. Most opposition to reform concerns more drug use by young people and greater threats to public safety if cannabis were more available. Concern for individual health has also been an issue.

Unlike the prohibitionist model, in which any and all illicit drug use constitutes abuse, the harm reduction perspective stresses education and responsible use over enforced abstinence. The pragmatic notion of treating drug use as fact, and moving on to deal with the problem of substance abuse in terms of relative harm, seems so inherently rational that one need not argue the point from any perspective other than simple 'common sense.' In the words of Robert Solomon, Professor of Law at the University of Western Ontario: "You don't need a theory. This is common sense, dumb as doorknobs. If you say what is the function of law? It seems to me that the function of law should respond to drugs, and our legal and regulatory response should reflect harm. If you jaywalk, do we put five officers on that? No. If you kill people we do. The whole legal system should be geared to protecting where the risks are greatest. And there's a hierarchy of risk starting with death and serious bodily injury, and you move down that scale. So it seems to me, in a sane society our approach to drugs should be geared to risk. Our laws would reflect the relative harm. Now exactly the opposite is true. We have invested huge amounts of energy and rigorous laws in areas where there is relatively little harm and ignored colossal harm in other areas."

Thus, carried to its logical conclusion, a rational approach to drug regulation would not only ease the restrictions on presently prohibited drugs; it would also tighten up restrictions on more harmful legal drugs like alcohol and tobacco. But in pro-prohibition rhetoric, the harms of marijuana and other illicit drugs have

53

long been grossly exaggerated. As Solomon explains, the drug establishment today still fosters the same "Miami Vice view of drugs" that was widely popularized in the 1980's. He argues: "The Miami Vice view of drugs is based on two myths...we hype the harms posed by the illicit drugs and we tell young people, every day in every way, that alcohol and tobacco are relatively benign. And if you look at the harms...much more harm is done by the second lie that alcohol and tobacco are relatively benign. Every day, every way, we tell young people that illicit drugs are horribly harmful and alcohol and tobacco are relatively benign, and that second lie kills tens of thousands of people a year in this country."

"And so what does that mean? That means that the Miami Vice view of drugs targets illicit drugs.... It doesn't target the advertising companies that do all the work for all the political parties, who happen to also do all the work for the tobacco and alcohol companies.... But if you want to see organized pushing of drugs, let's talk about the Canadian pharmaceutical industry where, with a small political campaign contribution, the patent drug people bought themselves a world of protection which cost us hundreds and hundreds of millions of dollars. So I guess when I look at it, I take a much broader view. I don't come to it from a particularly libertarian perspective...we can't start all over again. Any rational person starting all over again would prohibit tobacco. From a public health perspective you prohibit tobacco and you'd allow people to smoke marijuana. But you can't start all over again. I mean, I don't believe that we are going to move from the current state into rational drug scheduling based solely on physiological harm and societal costs. We're not going to do that."

"I don't think we can get from our current situation of prohibitionist mentality to legalization without going through decriminalization.... It's not that if one were to start all over again, one wouldn't necessarily want to ensure that our legal response to drugs was based on physiological effects and social costs. But we can't get there from where we are. What we have to see, at least in my view, is a coalescing, a movement away from criminal prohibition and illicit drugs on the one hand, and much, much tighter regulation of alcohol and tobacco on the other. I mean, I think the argument for much more rigorous regulation for tobacco and alcohol is overwhelming from a public health perspective. Libertarians may disagree, and I'm happy to have that. We in Canada believe that we would rather control things than people. In the United States you have free access to guns and then we spend all the money on the criminal justice system.... I'd rather control things than people. I think the state has a role in preventing harm. I'd be willing to regulate much more rigorously in the fields of alcohol and tobacco. A lot of libertarians wouldn't. We in Canada tend to adopt slightly different views."

As a call for harm reduction, or just plain "common sense," the excerpts from my interviews with Solomon and Single point to policy reforms that are relatively moderate, and thereby 'liberal' in some ways but not others. The ideological and practical implications of acquiring the liberal label are taken up in detail later on. It is sufficient here to note that from a prohibition standpoint, all drug policy reformers are characterized as liberal despite their efforts to attend to prohibitionist's concerns. Although firmly grounded in empirical evidence and the rational rhetoric of science, moderate proposals aiming for partial decriminalization, a legislative option for cannabis favoured by Solomon, Single, and other politically astute drug policy observers, remain nonetheless controversial. Several legislative options are examined here below. But first we take a closer look at public health discussions, with specific reference to harm reduction options for reducing harm to the user.

**Reducing Harm to the User:** In prohibitionist claims making, high potency, toxicity, and every possible behavioural aberration has been attributed to cannabis. With regard to potency, Morgan and his colleagues (Morgan et al. 1993, p. 218) note that while cannabis containing 0.05 percent by weight of its psychoactive agent (Delta-9-THC) is often judged effective, ten percent cannabis has been frequently reported. Status quo supporters argue that such potent material brings unwanted effects and greater toxicity; yet there is little evidence enhanced toxicity exists. Further, since smoked cannabis is easily titrated, since users receive cues about dosage because of the rapid onset of drug effects, smokers tend to inhale lower doses when presented with increasingly potent cannabis. In this light, it may be argued that enhanced potency is therefore an effective harm reduction strategy. In terms of toxicity, the available data suggest cannabis is a relatively harmless drug from a physical or life threatening perspective (Weppner and Inciardi 1978), thus supporting the oft-heard 'soft' versus 'hard' drug designation.

Although there is substantial disagreement about the physiological and psychological effects of cannabis, there is a general consensus that at usual levels of social usage the typical subjective effects include a sense of euphoria or well-being, with some reports of altered awareness and time perception. Physiological changes are relatively few and neurological examinations consistently reveal no major abnormalities during periods of intoxication. Death directly attributable to the drug's effects is extremely rare even at very high doses. Regarding the 'gateway' effect or the claim that marijuana use leads to harder drugs is not well founded, the frequent association between cannabis and tobacco may be an unrecognized cause for concern. For example, Solomon contends that: "One of my concerns with marijuana is that it's going to be a stepping stone, not to heroin, to tobacco. You have to learn how to inhale to smoke dope. The major public health fear in making marijuana more available is not that the marijuana is going to do harm.... My real fear is if we make it available, what we might find is it's a precursor to tobacco addiction which is devastatingly harmful. So I'm not convinced that we should make marijuana available. I am convinced that it is relatively innocuous. I worry about its consumption by way of smoking."

Since cannabis in Western cultures is predominantly consumed by way of combustion and inhalation, there is clearly some concern about the impact of its use on cardiopulmonary function. Morgan et al. (1993) note attempts to assess the impact of cannabis smoking on the lungs have been complicated by the concomitant use of tobacco by many users. It is important to emphasize that the pulmonary pathology described here is due not to the active ingredients of the drug, or cannabinoids, themselves but rather the inhalation of particulate material and toxins related to smoking. Whereas neither nicotine nor Delta-9-THC are pulmonary pathogens, there are dangers related to the concomitant inhalation of combusted plant material, which may lead to pulmonary inflammation and carcinogenesis. And whereas airway changes in heavy cannabis users are not those indicative of progression to the chronic obstructive pulmonary disease and emphysema of the tobacco smoker, the possibility of carcinogenic change remains (Morgan et al. 1993). Similar to smoking cigarettes, the repeated inhalation of combusted cannabis is damaging to the pulmonary system.

Under some system of reform, argue Morgan and his colleagues, the development of cannabis beverages, buccal lozenges, skin patches or other forms could be encouraged to diminish pulmonary hazards. Scientific studies exploring the uses of cannabis as a medicine, or recreational drug of choice, could take place and be used to inform public educational efforts aimed at reducing harm to the user. Of related interest with respect to calls for research, in March 1999 Canada announced that it would begin clinical trials on the medical use of marijuana. The move came two weeks prior to the public release of findings from a U.S. government funded study conducted by the National Academy of Sciences' Institute of Medicine. Finding against claims that it is a 'gateway,' addictive or otherwise harmful, the study gave guarded support for closely monitored medical use offset by specific warnings against smoked marijuana due to the risk of lung damage. Similarly, in Canada official acceptance for medical marijuana has been guarded at best, and continued proposals aimed at wider cannabis law reform are as hindered as ever by political realities.

Promoting harm reduction among drug users remains highly controversial for medical professionals and treatment service providers. Disseminating accurate public health information is thus a common task left to drug policy reformers. Since the risk of lung damage due to smoking is the most commonly claimed biological hazard, harm reduction calls for educational attempts to diminish customary practices such as deep inhalation and breath holding, which facilitates the deposition of particles without markedly increasing THC delivery, and the concurrent use of tobacco and cannabis by combustion (Morgan et al. 1993). Because THC is a bronchodilator it may augment the deleterious impact of tobacco smoking by abetting the deposition of particles deeper into respiratory airways. Considering the prevalence of cannabis consumption by way of combustion and inhalation in Western society, developing technology for THC delivery in a safer "smokeable" form is a goal worth pursuing from a public health standpoint. It is important to note that throughout recorded history people have used water pipes and other innovations to reduce damage to the lungs caused by cannabis smoking.

Such self-styled *harm reduction* strategies, often learned from other users, are actively promoted through a growing "cannabis culture" made possible in Canada, in part, along with the advent of the Internet, by the Supreme Court ruling to overturn Section 462.2 of the Criminal Code. From 1988 until the mid-1990's, when the law was ruled unconstitutional under the Canadian Charter of Rights and Freedoms, Section 462.2 effectively prohibited the manufacture, promotion and selling of all "instruments or literature for illicit drug use." Despite the continuation of police raids on "head shops" and other retail outlets carrying cannabis paraphernalia and literature, demonstrating an apparent refusal by law enforcers to heed the landmark ruling, the grass roots propagation of harm reduction technology is a significant public health development. Through the use of water pipes purchased in head shops, or home-made versions of them, although the claim remains debatable and in need of further research (see Zimmer and Morgan 1997), much of the tar and particulate matter found in marijuana smoke can be filtered out.

Moreover, by gently heating marijuana, so that the THC is vaporized and released but never reaches combustion temperature, inhaling carbon monoxide and other toxins is diminished, cutting the tar content to negligible amounts compared to smoke from a marijuana joint or tobacco cigarette. Morgan et al. (1993), for example, reported a study employing a heated copper filament to successfully deliver THC as a vapour to asthmatic subjects. The diffusion of vaporizer technology among recreational users has facilitated the development and marketing of several such devices based on much the same principle. As an underground enterprise that is just as illegitimate as the selling of water pipes and other cannabis paraphernalia, the safety and efficiency of all models available, however, should not be assumed. From a harm reduction standpoint, vaporizer manufacturers ought to be held to the same industry standards that regulate other electrical implements. It also follows that improvements in technology be encouraged to attain the optimum health benefits. The use of copper filament, for example as above, is not recommended because heated copper produces toxic fumes. The only safe material, according to a longtime manufacturer I met with, is brass, glass, or stainless steel. Despite attending risks to many uninformed consumers, such details are ignored in a prohibition framework because facilitating safe drug use is officially untenable.

By accepting cannabis use as a fact, harm reductionists argue, we might effectively address these issues through open communication and public educational efforts to diminish the more harmful aspects and practices. Significant changes in policy are crucial to this harm reduction schema. According to Morgan and his colleagues, for example: "Cannabis law reform is essential whether that reform is committed legalization, expiation or an enlightened hypocrisy in which existing laws are ignored. Such reform would save the large costs of cannabis law enforcement and could free criminal justice resources for focus on that which is proved harmful to the social community and public order.... Harm reduction also includes a commitment to education of youthful users in the character and perils of acute intoxication and acute cannabis effect. Some of the millions of Federal US dollars spent in promoting a futile prohibition and calling it education could be used to teach young people how to manage the effects safely" (Morgan et al. 1993, pp. 225-226). Thus, despite the common plea for political neutrality, which encourages us to come to strictly rational conclusions through empirically informed "cost-benefit" assessments, harm reduction options favour drug reform by default because inevitably they target problems caused by prohibition.

**Reducing Harm Due to Policy:** Policy recommendations from a cost-benefit perspective seek to minimize the health and safety risks accompanying drug use, while minimizing the social and personal costs of attempting to control users. The task of balancing social costs against the deterrent impact of the law has been increasingly reassessed, however, in light of the evidence on criminalization costs versus its presumed social benefits. Ever since a wave of liberal reforms in the 1970's effectively decriminalized recreational marijuana use in eleven U.S. states, drug policy analysts have amassed a sizeable body of evidence in support of these measures. Over a five-year period eleven states removed jail sentences for possession of small amounts of marijuana. The laws, collectively referred to as 'decriminalization,' generally specify that offenders are to be issued summons like those for traffic offenses rather than being taken into custody. The decriminalization 'movement' in the U.S. began in 1973 with Oregon, followed by Alaska, Maine, California, Colorado, and Ohio in 1975, Minnesota in 1976, Mississippi, New York, and North Carolina in 1977, and Nebraska in 1978. Although South Dakota enacted a decriminalization law in 1976, it never gained acceptance as a permanent part of the state's criminal code and was subsequently repealed. No states have decriminalized marijuana since 1978, and in 1990 Alaska 'recriminalized' the drug.

Thus, this wave of legislative reform, which for about one-third of Americans removed the threat of imprisonment for possessing small amounts of marijuana, has been largely dormant for over thirty years. The reform movement in the U.S., as in Canada, was revived in the 90's, as rallies to legalize marijuana increased in number and donations to the Washington office of NORML more than doubled (Redekop 1995). Changes to the federal drug laws over several administrations, of course, have not materialized. In Canada the legal status of the drug for recreational consumers remains largely unchanged since the 1969 Narcotic Control Act (NCA), which allocated the same penalties for possession of less than 30 grams of marijuana as those meted out for possession of physically addictive drugs that are generally agreed to be more harmful, such as heroin and cocaine. Though often classified as a depressant, there are important differences between cannabis (the Latin term for preparations made from the hemp plant, such as marijuana and hashish) and narcotic drugs, such as morphine and opium, or sedatives including alcohol and the barbiturates.

Most importantly, tolerance or physiological dependence on cannabis is held to be rare; that is, a person discontinuing its use does not undergo symptoms of withdrawal (Ebin 1961). The latest amendment to Canada's drug laws, the Controlled Drugs and Substances Act (CDSA) enacted in June 1996, puts cannabis in a separate category from 'hard drugs' like cocaine and heroin, but its criminal status is maintained, allowing for extraordinary powers of police search and seizure and the sentencing option of imprisonment for all possession offenses. Despite recommendations from drug policy experts, and even some talk to the press of including a cannabis decriminalization provision in the CDSA, the Senate Committee succeeded in passing what is essentially a revamped Narcotic Control Act with no major changes (Erickson 1998). To facilitate the framing of issues surrounding Canada's ongoing decriminalization debate, a selective review of the relevant literature appears in the section below.

**Criminalization Costs and Benefits:** The most obvious cost of marijuana prohibition for Canadians is the financial expense of enforcing the laws pertaining to simple possession. By the late 1970's, the crime of possessing small amounts of marijuana for personal use accounted for over one-tenth of adult charges, with an estimated cost to taxpayers of between 60 and 100 million dollars a year (Blackwell, Green, and Solomon 1979). The crime of possession diverts tremendous manpower and criminal justice resources from more serious crimes, while fostering hostility among marijuana offenders towards police and a legal system that subjects them to the indignity of arrest and the permanent stigma of a criminal record (Erickson 1980). The term 'criminal record' generally refers to any official account of a finding or plea of guilty and the sentence imposed. Once the accused appears in adult court, the charge becomes a matter of public record accessible to any Canadian police department, customs and immigration officials, or similar agencies. Whereas the majority of those arrested for possession receive only fines, with the percentage granted discharges increasingly steadily since the mid-1970's, all marijuana offenders regardless of the sentence imposed acquire a permanent criminal record with potentially devastating individual consequences.

Even those officially discharged or granted a pardon are at a distinct disadvantage in any subsequent criminal proceeding. Marijuana offenders may be denied entry into other countries and prevented from obtaining Canadian citizenship. Moreover, they may also find themselves severely limited in future job opportunities in both public and private sectors (Solomon, Single, and Erickson 1983). Equally troubling for many observers is the encroachment on individual rights and freedoms that are incurred in the enforcement of Canada's drug laws. The methods of enforcement used in drug investigations represent a marked departure from established principles of law governing the search of premises and their occupants. Officers are granted far broader powers of search and seizure in even a minor drug case, such as simple possession of marijuana, than they have in a murder, rape, arson, or other serious criminal case (Solomon et al. 1983). Policies facilitating law enforcement at the expense of established individual rights must certainly be considered a substantial social cost of the current drug laws, but they may be justified insofar as they presumably serve to discourage marijuana use.

The presumed benefit of criminal penalties for marijuana possession is its deterrent effect on use. Although it is difficult to estimate the deterrent effect of criminal penalties solely from trends in use, it is noteworthy that from the late 1960's up until the 1980's, when rates of use apparently began to level off, substantial increases in marijuana use occurred both in Canada and the U.S. despite the enforcement of very coercive measures. Consistent with research indicating that the law has a limited deterrent impact if the risk of detection and punishment is low (Teevan 1976), as is the case with marijuana use—it has been estimated that fewer than one percent of marijuana users are ever detected (LeDain 1972)—decreases in use, particularly among young people, have been linked to changing perceptions of health risks rather than the threat of legal sanctions (Single 1989). The experience of the eleven American states that have decriminalized marijuana possession provides further evidence of the law's limited deterrent effect.

Although the decriminalization states tended to have higher rates of marijuana use both before and after the changes in law, it was found that increases in use were even greater in other states, with the largest proportionate increases occurring in those states with the most severe penalties. Thus, as summarized by Single (1989), the available data suggest that decriminalization measures have had little or no impact on levels of use, while substantially reducing the social costs associated with the enforcement of marijuana laws. All of the decriminalization states experienced reductions in the number and nature of marijuana cases, with sharp declines in the incarceration of offenders and increased revenues from fines. In light of these data on U.S. experience, Canadian commentators have called for modifications in the marijuana laws ranging from outright nullification to full-scale government regulation and control of distribution. The range of possible alternatives is substantial, and related policy concerns are highly variable and complex. Drawing on the literature on different control structures, however, we can identify several broadly defined models that warrant consideration when discussing different options for reforming Canadian marijuana laws.

**Decriminalization Models and Theory**

Following Weppner and Inciardi (1978, pp. 123-24 italics in original), "...it can be postulated that contemporary marijuana legislation is based on the premise that *the State has the prerogative to evolve social policy in terms of the interest structure of society as a whole*...relative to the social impact of the *psychological and physiological costs* of marijuana use." The most important reason to repeal the prohibition of marijuana, writes Kaplan (1971, p. 312), "...is not that the drug is good but that the costs of criminalization are out of proportion to the benefits of this policy." Because criminal prohibitions involving private behaviour derive their legitimacy from congruence with more enduring normative precepts (Bonnie and Whitebread 1974), wherever these shared values are at variance with the law, the law must overextend

60

itself to enforce their provisions (Skolnick and Dombrink 1978). Public awareness of the inefficacy of law, which endangers both the moral authority of the social groups whose beliefs it symbolizes and the political authority of control agencies, can have a disastrous impact upon the law as an institution.

According to Scheerer (1978, p. 586), a legal system threatened by delegitimization can adapt to such a challenge in one of two ways. The first is through *criminalization* which serves to restore confidence in the existing normative order by means of increased penalties that eliminate the hard-core deviant while forcing others to conform to the conventional normative order. Criminalization is thereby defined as the creation of new moral boundaries within a social system, or the affirmation of existing ones, in an attempt to assimilate normative challenges. The other adaptation is *decriminalization* which accommodates the normative order to the challenging behaviour by adjusting moral boundaries to incorporate the deviant behaviour into the realm of normality. Although there is no real consensus on the meaning of the term decriminalization, Single (1989, p. 456) argues it should only be used to apply to behaviour which is not sanctioned by criminal law: "Thus, in evaluating the impact of 'decriminalization,' we are really only dealing with the impact of reducing penalties rather than the impact of removing penalties altogether."

With respect to marijuana, the term has generally been used to describe laws that reduce the legal sanctions for possession of small amounts to penalties other than imprisonment. In the so-called decriminalization states, for example, possession of marijuana is still against the law and subject to penalties, although the maximum penalty is only a fine. Even in the Netherlands, which amended the Opium Law in 1976 to decriminalize consumption of both hard and soft drugs while significantly increasing sanctions for large-scale dealing in illicit hard drugs, cannabis use is formally defined as a misdemeanour punished by a fine of 500 gilders or detention up to one month. This sanction is said to exist only on paper, however, since nonenforcement of the bill was officially intended from the start (Scheerer 1978). Thus the distinction between decriminalization and outright legalization is critical when evaluating the legislative potential of the following models.

*Nullification, Commodity Regulation, and Commercial Service Models.* As noted by Skolnick and Dombrink (1978), certain traditionally deviant or 'illegal' behaviours, including the use of various drugs other than marijuana, cocaine, and heroin, are already under control in our society with considerably less reliance upon the criminal law. At one extreme the "nullification" model, exemplified in the case of sexual relations between consenting adults, calls for the law to withdraw entirely from control of the activity with no alternative specified. This approach may seem inappropriate when applied to formerly criminal activities, but doing nothing is a viable alternative in many cases, so it remains a theoretical possibility and is not entirely without legal precedent. Providing for slightly greater control over substances like marijuana, the "commodity regulation" model maintains that the law should largely withdraw from the activity and enforce only minimal guarantees of quality and purity. Such models treat marijuana much like any other plant that can be freely used, grown in both private and commercial gardens, and sold like produce in a vegetable store (Skolnick and Dombrink 1978).

The commercial potential and other economic aspects of legalizing marijuana distribution tend also to support the "commercial service" model that is commonly applied in the case of legalized prostitution. This scenario, perhaps best exemplified by the brothels and 'coffee houses' of Amsterdam's famous red light district, while apparently viable in certain settings, brings to light important considerations regarding the regulation of private versus public consumption of goods and services. As with the consumption of food in public restaurants, for example, government regulations on the sale of recreational drugs or sex between consenting adults may actually offer a purer case of 'control' than prohibition. Thus, according to Skolnick and Dombrink (1978, p. 202, italics mine): "The private kitchen can be unwashed. But when the public is charged a price for the privilege of eating, consumer protection norms formalized into law propel the state into an obligation to inquire whether the kitchen is clean. Although it does not follow as day from night, ordinarily *legalization of commercial services provokes regulation*."

Government controls over the marijuana market, through the provision of a legally regulated source of supply, could range from general systems of taxation or licensing to highly restrictive regimes in which all aspects of production and distribution are directly controlled by the government. Another alternative to strict government regulation is the 'medical' distribution model.

*Government Regulation and Medical Models.* The medical model often proposed as an alternative approach to narcotics control implies a drastic change from the current drug laws insofar as illicit drugs like marijuana, cocaine, and heroin would be redefined according to their various properties and sold like any other drug under a doctor's prescription. Conclusions from the British experience with medicalizing heroin addiction are compelling. It has been noted, for example, that medically endorsed addicts are perceived differently than those produced by a drug subculture. At the same time a medical drug control model is also portrayed as a highly complex system with new problems generated by the solution (Skolnick and Dombrink 1978). Although many physicians may favour some sort of decriminalization of recreational drug use, medical professionals have been divided on the criteria for prescribing marijuana. As a consequence it follows that the majority do not wish to bear professional responsibility for such treatment. Unlike with physically addicting narcotic drugs as well, it may be difficult for doctors to justify prescribing marijuana to 'dependent' users out of a concern for the patient's health. The use of cannabis as medicine further complicates the issue with respect to the involvement of physicians in dispensing to non-medical consumers of the drug.

Government licensing and distribution schemes are complex also and come with an array of

62

difficulties of their own. Given its broad discretionary powers and procedural formalities, government licensing of legalized vice represents a highly developed form of modern bureaucracy. According to Skolnick and Dombrink (1978), the use of state power to assess, define, and manage the economics of a formerly deviant activity is further complicated by the social purpose of decriminalization and licensing. The movement towards licensed casino gambling in North America and Great Britain, for example, demonstrates that decriminalization can serve quite different social purposes. Whereas Nevada licenses casino gambling primarily to produce income for the state, and struggling tourist resorts like Niagra Falls and Atlantic City have introduced casinos to renew their popularity, Britain, by contrast, views gambling as a social problem that needs to be regulated so as *not* to stimulate demand. Despite several unique advantages—particularly the substantial revenues generated, ability to ensure purity and limit the potency of the drug, and reduction in criminal activity arising from large-scale trafficking—government regulation of marijuana distribution poses some serious problems (Solomon et al. 1983).

Although available studies have found no significant increases in marijuana use following decriminalization, government regulation still represents a fundamental shift in policy that may be interpreted by the public as advocating use of the drug. Schemes that are similar but more restrictive than the provincial alcohol distribution systems, with features like consumer licensing, rationed sales, limited hours of operation, and proof-of-age requirements, are attractive in theory but also raise a number of constitutional problems. Since public attitudes towards the drug may vary from province to province, for example, attempting to establish a marijuana distribution system within the provinces would be contentious and politically volatile (Solomon et al. 1983). Such an approach would also require Canada to withdraw from at least some of the provisions of the Single Convention on Narcotic Drugs, a formal international treaty obligation that has been in effect since 1961. As noted by Scheerer (1978), this obligation prevented the Dutch government from legalizing cannabis in 1976, deflecting them instead towards a misdemeanour solution, one of several legislative innovations to employ a 'vice model' approach to marijuana reform. Several features of this model are discussed below, with additional reference to 'de facto decriminalization' or selective non-enforcement of the law.

*The Vice Model and De facto Decriminalization.* Conforming closely with the criminalization model, the vice model has long been considered the most politically feasible model for marijuana decriminalization (Skolnick and Dombrink 1978). Under this solution, selling or trafficking in marijuana remains criminal but, as in many gambling and prostitution cases, the mere customer or user is freed completely from any threat of criminal punishment. The 'fine only' option practiced in ten U.S. states, for example, attempts to mitigate the negative effects of criminalization by eliminating incarceration as a sentencing option for simple possession offenses. Other mitigation alternatives range from a modest lowering of maximum penalties to more elaborate schemes that would reduce penalties, simplify criminal procedures, and prevent the creation of a permanent criminal record (Solomon et al. 1983). Whereas the adverse consequences of a criminal record can be reduced, however, they cannot be eliminated. As long as marijuana possession remains a criminal offence, its enforcement will generate volumes of data—much of which the federal government cannot control—and involve complex legislation that contributes to widespread public confusion about the marijuana laws. Moreover, as long as sellers are criminalized, there can be no controls on the quality and kinds of drugs they sell, and illegal selling will continue to serve as an entry point for many people into a ready distribution market (Skolnick and Dombrink 1978).

Since they are not designed to reduce the number of people criminalized for marijuana offenses, the mitigation alternatives are illogical when viewed from a cost-benefit standpoint. By comparison there are clear advantages to gain from a partial repeal of the possession offence that would eliminate the social costs and adverse individual consequences of criminalizing marijuana use. Since very few first offenders are now imprisoned for marijuana possession, the fine-only option does not represent a major change in policy. Although such options may reduce at least some of the costs of enforcing prohibition, "...even the most comprehensive mitigation proposals would affect only the extent and not the fact of criminalization" (Solomon et al. 1983, p. 431). A partial repeal that reduces the scope of the possession offence—exempting from liability at least some consumption related behaviours for those in possession of less than one ounce, for example, or permitting home cultivation for personal use—would allow users to avoid involvement in the illegal market and drastically reduce the number of people criminalized. Moreover, it could be argued that the partial repeal alternative is compatible with a government policy of discouraging marijuana use.

According to Solomon and his colleagues: "The government could attempt to reduce the safety risks involved in cannabis use by creating special offenses and enforcement programs to deal with consumption in high-risk situations...public use or even display of cannabis could be prohibited...and similar legislative proposals could be coupled with public information programs related to the health and safety risks of cannabis use (Solomon et al. 1983, p. 429). Compared to the mitigation alternatives, including the practice of *de facto decriminalization*, the partial repeal option is straightforward and logical. Nevertheless, as in many other areas of the law, legal reform is not so much the result of rational analysis as it is a reflection of legislative innovation embedded in a history of legal rules and social symbols: "The definitional and political character of social problems is paramount" (Skolnick and Dombrink 1978, p. 203). This point is often overlooked by analysts who argue for reforming drug policies on 'rational' grounds such as the unenforceability of the law or its lack of deterrence.

Since the upholders of law are given assurance that their way of life is correct, support for the law is rooted in emotional and symbolic worlds that are not subject to future-oriented, rational arguments (Johnson and Newmeyer 1975). Today's preponderance of de facto decriminalization over actual reform reflects the symbolic power of criminal penalties, even if unenforced. Although the real differences between actual and de facto legislation for law enforcement and most marijuana users are not that great, the latter has obvious symbolic advantages for legislators, who are seldom interested in taking political risks: "Since law enforcement has only finite resources, if legislatures refuse to set law enforcement priorities, police will do it for them" (DiChiara and Galliher 1994, p. 73). Shifting the focus from drug control models that have been proposed for marijuana law reform, the following discussion is concerned with exploring drug reform claims making in its broader cultural context.

Social and Political Conditions: Public support for legal restraints on private morality is one of the more enduring legacies of our Puritan heritage, reflecting a history of forced self-restraint in the lower-middle class, and resentment towards illicit drug users and other seekers of "unearned pleasures" (Johnson and Newmeyer 1975). Consumer abundance and economic cushioning, from unemployment insurance and social security, have made many traditional Puritan values obsolete. Whereas the pursuit of pleasure is permissible, however, it is argued that the pleasure must be 'earned.' Transgressors are more likely to be resented if perceived as foreshadowing a trend towards diminishing controls. With the significance of economic scarcity declining as a control on behaviour, legal restraints, although ineffective and often unenforceable, have become an alternative source of control. Demographic changes in the typical marijuana user over the past forty years—i.e., rising use among middle-class, college-educated whites—have intensified enforcement difficulties, providing the social context for drug policy reform.

Rising middle-class drug use is associated with a trend of increasing individualism in Western industrial society. In a heterogeneous or "loosely bounded" culture, people will adopt more private versions of self through a rhetoric of individual freedom and choice (Gamson 1992, p. 87) which allows for greater tolerance of alternative lifestyles and more pragmatic forms of social control. The assumption of free choice, however, may be problematic when applied to youth and the lower classes. It has been argued, for example, that socially disadvantaged youth are more vulnerable to drug abuse because alternative and satisfying drug-free lifestyles are less available to them. According to De Leon (1982, p. 48): "It is not unreasonable to assume that changes in the conduct and values of the middle class, particularly with respect to recreational drug use, could negatively influence the adjustment of the socially disadvantaged. A middle class that appears to emphasize leisure, self-indulgence, or momentary gratification confuses the values of earned achievement and undermines the importance of self-discipline."

While such arguments are patronizing, and likely overstated, class differences may warrant more attention from researchers concerned about the impact of marijuana decriminalization. More to the present point, in Scheerer's (1978, pp. 601-602) comparison of the Dutch and German drug laws, he notes that

German society, with its high degree of cultural, ethnic, and religious homogeneity, "...is relatively high on formal control and low in its capacity to adapt to emerging social change." By contrast, "...in a heterogeneous society like that of the Netherlands, government is possible only through compromise, adaptability, and pragmatism...." In a heterogeneous society, by keeping political participation by the masses indirect, *interest group liberalism* encourages a political culture of moderation and compromise through the mediating mechanisms of pluralism that protect us from the tyranny of majority rule. Unlike the populist notion that the people should rule directly in their own best interests, pluralism emphasizes "...controlled negotiation among leaders of interest groups with a stake in decisions" (Gamson 1992, p. 138). Thus, in essence, the interest groups *are* the people in a heterogeneous society.

But while these points may be supported by Scheerer's (1978) explanation of successful decriminalization efforts in the Netherlands versus Germany, they are less convincing with respect to the U.S. Although the heterogeneity hypothesis appears to apply in demographically diverse decriminalization states with large urban populations, like New York and California, other states such as Nebraska and Maine are sparsely populated and relatively homogeneous. Similarly, some of these states (e.g., Minnesota and Oregon) are well-known liberal enclaves, but others (e.g., Mississippi and North Carolina) are conservative, and every region of the nation is represented (DiChiara and Galliher 1994). Considering the range of demographic differences among the states that passed marijuana decriminalization laws, the search for determinant factors shifted toward more specific political conditions and associated strategies of influence. Because the American public, like Canadians, have been evenly divided on the issue of marijuana reform, a stalemate situation had arisen where the role of political leaders and organized interest groups became increasingly relevant.

DiChiara and Galliher (1994) note a number of political strategies that were employed in the decriminalization states to shift the balance in the direction of reform. Whereas public ambivalence made marijuana decriminalization a legitimate issue, legislative success was dependent on "narrow policy windows" (Kingdon 1995) wherein the moral panics that politicized the issue were avoided by increasing the visibility of instrumental advantages. In rural states like Nebraska, Minnesota, and North Carolina, for example, decriminalization measures were already in practice due to limited resources, and there was little public or legislative interest in trying to enforce the marijuana laws. Instrumental advantages, such as cost efficiency and protecting the young from criminal penalties, were particularly visible in those states where decriminalization never became a critical political issue simply because the existing marijuana laws were not routinely enforced.

According to DiChiara and Galliher (1994, p. 58), the lack of intense political conflict in legislative proceedings behind the majority of marijuana decriminalization bills demonstrates that in America

"...routinization was the key to success." When marijuana reforms were not presented in a routine manner, the initiatives always failed. In some states the failure of marijuana reforms was a consequence of how the issue was originally framed. Initiatives violating the narrow boundaries of successful decriminalization legislation inevitably failed. In no case did proposals calling for the outright legalization of possession, or allowing the cultivation or sale of marijuana, meet with majority approval. Successful reforms are both narrowly circumscribed and respectful of the message that marijuana use is improper. Wide-ranging liberal bills, seeking legalization of all drugs, prostitution, gay rights, and abortion on demand, for example, have suffered a considerable mortality rate.

In the case of marijuana policy reform, diversionary tactics, such as toughening other drug laws or clamping down on dealers so as not to appear soft on crime, are often necessary for survival. Indeed, it has been argued that the key to decriminalization is actually held by the moral conservatives of society. So says Scheerer (1978, p. 590), for example: "Even if the initiative for decriminalization is taken by liberals, it will be the moral center that determines it success. Yet the powerful organizations of the moral conservatives are still not entirely free in choosing the direction of legal change. The decision to criminalize or decriminalize is dependent on the activities of organized interest groups and the position of government officials." While the efforts of opposing interest groups often cancel each other out, conservative sponsoring of decriminalization initiatives may be crucial to their success, allowing liberal interest groups to maximize opportunities for collective action.

In the 1970's in the U.S., the only national organization lobbying for marijuana decriminalization (NORML) built upon the support of a few Republican politicians by mobilizing their resources—which included the media and a group of respected academics, doctors, and lawyers who spoke out in favour of reform—to influence public opinion and decision making at key legislative hearings (Anderson 1981). Policy windows open infrequently, however, and do not stay open long. Failed proposals are seldom followed up as vigorously, and changes in political leadership often make them less feasible. The advent of the Reagan years in the 1980's, for example, precipitated an intensification of the 'war on drugs,' the emergence of a 'new right' movement in American politics, and general changes in the "national mood" (Kingdon 1995) of the people regarding recreational drug use. By the end of the 1970's, the reform efforts of groups like NORML were increasingly countered by concerned parents groups and other interests who had gained influence and a sympathetic ear in Washington.

Thirty years later, despite its strategic grounding in the rational language of harm reduction and politically neutral arguments for reform, marijuana law reform today continues to countered by cultural conservatives in much the same fashion. Of some relevance to harm reduction's prospects for acceptance in the Canadian political context, the influence of American drug war ideology on global policy conventions

67

has been well documented (see Giffen, Lambert, and Endicott 1991). When asked to identify the key factors opposing cannabis reform in Canada, a majority of participants in the present study noted the global impact of American drug policy. The following statement by Bruce Alexander, a Professor of Psychology at Simon Fraser University, is suggestive of the general tone. When asked about the potential for cannabis policy changes in Canada, he said: "I don't think you can talk about it independently of the United States...drug war is an instrument of international policy for them which they rely on, and they've used it over and over and over again in order to achieve various kinds of international goals, and they can't let go of it. And they therefore can't let us let go of it, and we've got basically chicken-shit governance that won't do anything to offend them too much, and I think that is the reality at the moment unfortunately."

"...it's not just a matter of simply evolving a national policy that would make sense. I think Canada, in my grasp of it, is perfectly able to do what the Dutch have done which is gradually evolve towards a more sensible policy notwithstanding certain kinds of international conventions. You can just evolve a reasonable policy. We're doing it in Vancouver. Nobody's being too offended...people are doing the same thing more quietly and the police are going to great lengths not to bother them, and they should be doing that. And so I think we're perfectly capable of change in a positive way, but I don't think we're going to be allowed to in the current international realities. Now of course I'm guessing about the American motives but I think, if there's sufficient material on it, it would be quite self-evident that they use it over and over again to achieve various international goals, to control Panama, for example, to enlist support in Nicaragua. They need this drug war and they intend to maintain it, and they will in spite of the transparent problems with it. I think we only have a certain amount of latitude."

"...I want to understand it in those larger international terms because I don't think it can be understood locally. More local, I think we would handle it. I think the anthropology that I know says to me that little cultures can handle drugs perfectly well. They ban some, they allow others; they ritualize some, they demonize others, and that's fine. Everyone's more or less happy because it's done in a way which makes sense in that culture. And I think Canada is perfectly capable of doing that too, but the international milieu is where the ultimate problem lies." Professor Alexander links the American influence to a larger "temperance mentality" that continues to dominate drug policy discussions, thereby limiting the scope of rational arguments for reform. Harm reduction's claims to value neutrality notwithstanding, it has had little influence on policy discussions due to contradictions in philosophical outlook. These contentions are developed more in chapter four with reference to discursive limitations of the harm reduction movement and associated challenges for cannabis reform.

**Summary**

Although respect for civil liberties is integral to harm reduction, the political issue of drug use as a basic human right is avoided in favour of cost-benefit analyses that are claimed to be morally neutral. Harm reduction eschews moral challenges to prohibition in favour of strictly rational arguments for reform. Unlike policy recommendations for heroin and other more dangerous drugs, which tend to focus on reducing the risk of personal harm due to use, harm reduction options for marijuana tend to focus on lowering the cost of enforcing drug laws which have failed to deter recreational use. By easing legal restrictions prohibiting simple possession and use of cannabis, it is argued that even partial decriminalization would substantially lower the cost of enforcement and mitigate the personal impact of imposing criminal sanctions on users. While only on the books in a few U.S. states, such measures are already employed in practice in many North American jurisdictions. Current examples in Canada range from court ordered 'diversion' or alternative sentencing for non-violent cannabis offenders to the pattern of selective non-enforcement often practiced by police in larger cities like Vancouver.

Developments resembling de facto decriminalization indicate pragmatic acceptance for the idea that rather than designing a better system, it is better in practice to muddle along using existing systems. This approach suggests a kind of "deliberate and constructive sloppiness" that has been attributed to the Dutch model (Mugford 1993, p. 31n). Enacting actual reforms to allow health service providers to actively promote harm reduction for drug users remains a highly controversial matter. Under blanket prohibition, promoting harm reduction measures is often left to advocates with no option but to operate outside the scope of law at the sufferance of police. The official implementation of harm reduction based programming for illicit drugs in Canada is still far from inevitable. In the context of existing sociopolitical conditions, including geographical proximity to the U.S. and continuing adherence to the temperance tradition, the ban on marijuana and other illicit drug use is certain to persist into the foreseeable future. In the further light of insights from informants in this study, in chapter four we take a closer look at the discursive limitations of the modern harm reduction movement.

## CHAPTER FOUR
## HARM REDUCTION RHETORIC
## AND THE LIMITS OF RATIONAL DISCOURSE[*]

There are important practical and philosophical concerns that limit the effectiveness of harm reduction rhetoric. Promoting a morally neutral, middle-ground conception of the drug problem, harm reduction addresses the matter of harm due to abuse rather than drug use *per se*. However, seeking rational solutions based on 'cost-benefit' analysis narrows the scope of harm reduction in practice, bringing to light ideological inconsistencies and rhetorical limitations of the public health perspective. Despite its logical appeal, the language of harm reduction ultimately prevents its proponents from saying what they really mean in support of humane policies and civil liberties. Whereas respect for civil liberties is integral to harm reduction, moral warrants upholding social norms of tolerance and the human rights of drug users are downplayed in favour of empirical analyses that are claimed to be morally neutral. But since the only benefit that can be counted where illicit drug use is concerned is 'pleasure,' something that is difficult to defend in the rational discourse of harm reduction (Mugford 1993), we are left with a one-sided analysis of cost that undervalues pleasure, reflecting western culture's modern temperance tradition.

Since the language and logic of 'harm reduction' has obvious appeal for a wide range of drug abuse practitioners and programs, there has been cooption by some status quo supporters who favour total abstinence as the goal of treatment. Here some limitations of harm reduction are examined with reference to both sides of the cannabis debate. First we look at problems due to cooption of the language and difficulties

---

[*] Portions of this chapter have been previously published in Hathaway, A.D. 2001. Shortcomings of Harm Reduction: Toward a Morally Invested Drug Reform Strategy. International Journal of Drug Policy 12(2): 125-137.

stemming from its politically astute yet philosophically conflicted tendency to replicate endangerment style rhetoric. These are illustrated with particular attention to drug education and the issue of 'drugged driving.' More generally—returning to the problem of excluding drug use benefits and other contradictions impeding the perspective—I conclude, with Nadelmann (1993), that harm reduction's greatest challenge lies in the promotion of its underlying ideals which adherents tend to overlook.

**Practical and Political Problems**

As a matter of strategy harm reductionists claim political neutrality. Harm reduction takes the middle road between right wing prohibitionists and anarchic libertarians, staking out the common ground shared by pro-legalization advocates and "progressive prohibitionists" (Nadelmann 1993). Nadelmann points out that there are tactical advantages to adopting harm reduction as a slogan or policy label: "Who, in their right mind, could oppose the notion of reducing harm? It is easily embraced by government officials and others who favor less emphasis on criminal justice policies and more emphasis on public health approaches, and not readily disavowed even by those who prefer more punitive drug control measures. It is sufficiently vague that people with very different ideas about drug policy feel comfortable adopting it as their label. And it conveys a sense of British or Dutch 'sensibility' that can prove irresistible to those who view the ideological excesses of drug war rhetoric with a sceptical eye" (p. 37).

The common ground between prohibitionists and legalizers is significant, he continues, for it suggests "...there is a basic framework of analysis, predicated upon systematic assessment of costs and benefits, that is regarded as intellectually legitimate by all serious analysts of drug control policy" (p. 43), one that cannot be negated despite value differences and the wide range of ideological assumptions at stake. Whereas the "wonderfully neutral" language of harm reduction has made significant inroads in Europe and Australia, however, the same language has failed to take hold in the United States (Nadelmann 1993). In North America harm reduction has been vulnerable to debasement by groups that favour criminalizing substance users and treatment programs that treat them as diseased and in need of curative abstinence. Eric Single stated that: "The harm reduction movement now is in sort of an identity crisis due to definitional issues...which is much more than a semantic. It's in danger in many places of being coopted by abstinence oriented interventions like criminalizing users, abstinence oriented treatment, so there's different conceptualizations of how harm reduction sprang up."

72

He continued, "I was at an AIDS conference in the States where the Minister of Health in the U.S. got up and started talking about throwing people in jail as a harm reduction measure, and that would be very much against what the notion of harm reduction is about to the people who started the harm reduction movement. So there's a big issue over do you include abstinence oriented strategies or don't you. For example, Australia's national drug strategy is based nominally on harm reduction principles, but in Canada it became defined as anything being used in favour of drug reform, which includes twelve step programs and criminalizing the user, and Australia didn't include those things. So nominally they were both harm reduction, but very different in terms of the kinds of programs they funded. It's still very much an issue.... Ideally, you should have an empirical definition to determine if it actually does reduce harm or not, but there are a lot of practical problems and much of the data regarding social stigma and things like that are not easily quantifiable...you have to maintain a larger all encompassing definition."

"But you should establish some principles to provide some initial direction, because if you include abstinence under the rubric of harm reduction, then the problem is that you've included everything and it provides you with no way to prioritize things. It's an important issue because there are places where harm reduction is starting to peter out.... In many places it's been coopted by abstinence oriented approaches, and until they come to an agreement within harm reduction about what it is and what it isn't, that danger of cooptation is very, very strong. ...harm reduction has nothing to say about long term goals of intervention, so it has nothing against abstinence oriented intervention. Because very often harm reduction is the first step in getting people to get off drugs.... So I'm trying to defuse the situation a little bit by means of modified empirical definitions—on the basis of probabilities, does it reduce harm? But there's no one satisfactory answer. Ultimately, what we need is better data—so we can answer the question 'Is a particular policy really reducing harm or not?'—to be able to move from a narrow definition to an empirically based one."

The problem with harm reduction, in Single's estimation, is partly political and partly technical. Putting the emphasis on technical problems and the need for 'better data,' harm reductionists hold fast to the notion that the main impediments to rational debate are empirically resolvable. With regard to cannabis and harm reduction, Single stated law reform may be inevitable after the more prominent practical issues are resolved. He argues: "The whole problem with harm reduction with cannabis is that the specific harms associated with cannabis have never been identified. I mean the potential ones have, but as for the actual rates at which they occur there's no good evidence, given the millions of users, of the health problems caused. That

73

doesn't mean it's a benign drug, but there's a tendency to measure harm caused by cannabis by cannabis use rates."

"I think a harm reduction perspective when it's applied to cannabis means that you should be focusing on the specific harms caused by cannabis as the dependent variable of analysis. What is the problem? Well, it's not use *per se*; it's the harm associated with use...focusing on harms rather than use per se wouldn't necessarily all be in a direction favouring drug reform, but it would allow us to target harm better. What I really dislike about prohibition is that it's so poorly targeted.... I don't mind interventions *per se*, but they don't allow you to focus on harm. It's the easy way out, make it illegal, and often there are worse consequences or just as many negative consequences as positive ones. We don't know enough to have a target, so we've been sort of stuck with this policy of prohibition. The harm reduction perspective focuses more on the specific harms in the hope of focusing interventions so you don't have to have this blanket prohibition."

The public safety issue of driving while intoxicated and adolescent drug use are objections often uttered in debates on marijuana law reform. The predominance of claims making that feeds the public fear of endangerment from substance use, especially by youth, has illustrative practical and political implications. Considering its emphasis in policy discussions, there is a lack of systematic research and neglect of recent studies about cannabis and driving. This is an impediment to harm reduction interventions that reflects political dimensions of a problem found in many areas of science research funding. Some of the challenge is political and some of it is technical, and some relates to the existing disciplinary structure of institutional, professional, and academic interests.

Single argues, for example: "Partly it's the cost of expertise, and the expertise you have tends to come from a certain perspective, like a medical background. They're not interested in these other aspects of research. That's one of the problems. It's very hard to get anything off the draft table because the research boards are dominated by psychologists and M.D.s, so it's much safer to publish these innocuous experiments. It's much easier to get money to run rats than it is to explore policy options through these studies and all the aspects surrounding drug use.... I've sat on those boards.... They don't understand ethnographers intentionally don't start with hypotheses because they depend so much on their observations; they don't want to be coloured by *a priori* definitions. I think we have to be a little more open to less hard science and more innovative research designs. But I don't see it as a conspiracy, not at all...".

74

Despite paradigmatic resistance to innovative research and programming, harm reductionists generally maintain that rational reform is inevitable pending technical advancement and diffusion of empirical knowledge. Given adequate funding for research and the accumulation of systematic data based on cost-benefit analysis, it is generally expected that policy changes to allow better targeting of drug-related harm will eventually follow. But from a status quo perspective, the costs of prohibition are presumably outweighed by the benefits that follow from the deterrent impact of the law. Any loosening of restrictions that might increase availability would increase the risk of public endangerment and send the wrong message to Canada's youth.

**Drug Education, Driving, and the Risk of Endangerment:** As noted above, the available data from American states that have decriminalized marijuana suggest little impact on levels of use, but a large reduction in the cost of law enforcement. Decreases in cannabis consumption, particularly among young people, have been linked to changing perceptions of health risks rather than the threat of legal sanctions (Single 1989). In this light, harm reduction favours drug use education that targets harmful practices of those whose use continues over more coercive interventions. But enduring resistance to drug education being *about* as opposed to *against* drugs, and other policy alternatives to criminalizing users, shows that the perceived threat of endangerment is still the most prominent obstacle to legal reform. Despite opposing evidence, dire adverse consequences presumably thus follow looser cannabis restrictions and official tolerance of users. Emphasizing the reduction of drug related harm negates themes of autonomy and tolerance of users by conceding risk assessment as the overarching framework.

As a matter of strategy, harm reduction abandons the contentious moral issue of the right to use drugs by engaging with opponents in the rhetoric of endangerment, while rejecting prohibition as the necessary solution. Although the core assumptions of harm reduction interventions respect the individual's right to exercise free will, with emphasis on accurate and credible information to promote responsible behaviour, the one-sided focus on harm is at odds with this pragmatic stance. Harm reduction education would, in theory, recognize that there are costs and benefits of drug use, and be respectful of the motivation and decision to use drugs. As described by Erickson (1997, pp. 1397-98), for example: "This approach acknowledges the appeal of drug use from the young person's perspective as well as its potential medical, social and legal consequences. It is rooted in an appreciation of adolescent psychosocial development, in which curiosity, a willingness to experiment and the definition of personal boundaries come into play. Thus, the more general

75

educational aim of developing the young person's capacity for autonomous decision-making is extended to the issue of drug use."

Indeed, it has been argued that experimental drug use is a normal expression of adolescent development and that experimenters are psychologically healthier than either abstainers or more frequent users (Shedler and Block 1990). Although such arguments concur with a harm reduction stance suggesting efforts to eliminate adolescent experimentation will be overly costly and meet with limited success, they are anathema to the standard education and prevention programs premised on a dichotomy of choices between abstinence and abuse. Traditionally, the only legitimate option where illicit drugs are concerned has been abstinence. Maintaining credibility among policy makers thereby requires the tempering of claims about drug use having benefits to stay within the acceptable parameters of the therapeutic model. The following disclaimer by Shedler and Block (1990, p. 628) is illustrative of the professional tendency to concede the conventional wisdom on drug use.

To fend off any misinterpretation of their findings, the authors dutifully acknowledge that: "The finding that experimenters are the psychologically healthiest adolescents, and the observation that some drug experimentation, in and of itself, does not seem to be psychologically destructive, may sit badly with some. In particular, it may sit badly with drug counselors who 'know' from clinical experience that there is no level of drug use that is safe, that it is dangerous to suggest otherwise, and that the most effective intervention is one aiming at total abstinence. To avoid any misunderstanding, we wish to make clear that there is no contradiction between this therapeutic perspective and the findings we have reported. On the contrary, we are in agreement with the therapeutic perspective." They go on to assert that experimentation with drugs is highly destructive for some adolescents and categorically deny any interpretation of their findings as indicating that drug use might somehow improve psychological health.

The question of drug use having possible benefits is ultimately precluded, much as it is in harm reduction perspective, by an overarching concession to the dominant paradigm. Though harm reduction has made inroads as a viable health strategy, its full integration into drug education programs requires "...a paradigm shift, from the 'problem of use,' as viewed by adults, to the 'problems with use,' as experienced by adolescents" (Poulin and Elliott 1997, p. 1392). Despite the call for evidence to evaluate harm reduction education in comparison to more traditional approaches, any resolution will require that adolescents, health professionals, parents, and educators come to terms with their values concerning adolescent drug use (Poulin and Elliot 1997). Returning to the issue of cannabis and driving, another so-called 'empirical problem,' assessments of harm relate far more to cultural values than empirical reasoning will allow.

Much of the evidence to date suggests that marijuana has a much less negative impact on driving than alcohol. Under experimental conditions, THC's effects on driving performance never exceed those of alcohol at concentrations beyond the legal limit and are in no way unusual compared to many medications. Further, notes Robbe (1997, p. 136): "...THC's effects differ qualitatively from many other drugs, especially alcohol. Evidence from the present and previous studies strongly suggests that alcohol encourages risky driving whereas THC encourages greater caution, at least in experiments. Another way THC seems to differ qualitatively from many other drugs is that the former's users seem better able to compensate for its adverse effects while driving under the influence." THC's adverse effects on driving performance appear to be relatively small, he concludes, though one can easily imagine driving situations where using cannabis might be dangerous—in emergencies, for example, or when taken with other drugs, especially alcohol. An important practical implication of the study is the finding that nothing conclusive can be surmised about a driver's impairment on the basis of THC concentrations in the bloodstream.

Whereas educational efforts aimed at promoting drug safety may wish to discourage impaired driving under any conditions, particularly by young adult males and other high risk groups, the driving performance of cannabis users in large part comes down to personal experience. The ability to control or regulate drug use is more than a matter of limiting the amount of drugs consumed. Ultimately, users themselves regulate their use of intoxicants through a process of learning in which specific rituals and rules are developed as adaptations to the effects of interaction between drug, set and setting (Zinberg 1984). Under the dominant canopy of prohibitionist rhetoric, however, any notion of controlled drug use, despite its empirical grounding in social learning theory, is as heretical as the idea of drug use having benefits. Past research on the use of interpretive strategies in constructing the drunk driving problem in America (see Gusfield 1981, 1988 and McCarthy 1994) is cited for its relevance to the present work below.

*Creating the Drunk Driver.* In the United States prior to 1960, if there was any common public understanding of automobile accidents at all, driver error was the dominant attributed cause (Nader 1972). By the mid-1960's, however, based on the claims of a loosely connected group of professional reform advocates and bureaucrats, a very different understanding of automobile accident causes began to emerge. The essence of the argument was that improvements in automobile design, including improved tire and brake quality, seat

77

belts, air bags, and safety glass, can reduce the likelihood of injury and death by making crashes less likely and minimizing the consequences of accidents that do occur. In summarizing the policy agenda of the new auto safety frame, Nader (1972) observed that whereas the tragic toll on the highway can hardly be disputed, the interpretation of this tragedy remains the primary obstacle to a more rational selection of safety strategies and their implementation. As cited in Gusfield (1988, p. 115): "The aim should be to have the automobile industry produce an automobile under the assumption that fools and drunks would drive it."

According to a prominent auto safety reformer: "There is not much evidence that the number of accidents can be substantially reduced simply by altering the behavior of drivers...the most efficient way to minimize the overall cost of accidents is to design the interior of the vehicles so that the *injuries* that follow the *accidents* are relatively mild. An attraction of this approach is that it could be put into effect by changing the behavior of a tiny population—the forty or fifty executives who run the automobile industry" (Moynihan 1966, p. 12, italics in original). To promote this new frame, a small band of highly educated reformers coalesced around Nader to focus attention on changing the behaviour of vehicle manufacturers who had been notoriously inattentive to safety concerns. As noted by McCarthy (1994), proponents of the auto safety frame were very successful in bringing it to public attention during the mid-1960's. In 1966, in the professional reform tradition that has become typical of American policy making (Lowi 1969), a new federal agency, which later became known as the National Highway Traffic Safety Administration (NHTSA), was created to carry out a progressive program of auto safety reform.

The goals of that reform centred on improving vehicle design rather than driver performance as the appropriate strategy to ameliorate the consequences of automobile crashes. Whereas attention to auto safety held steady into the late 1970's, however, the agency's efforts to create and enforce safety standards have been strongly resisted by auto manufacturers. After 1980, yet another frame for understanding automobile crash-related injury and death rapidly gained prominence, that of the "drunken driver." McCarthy (1994) looked at several other frames that have been elaborated to explain automobile accidents. One of them stresses the disproportionate involvement of young males in automobile crashes (as is found in serious crime of all kinds). Another frame, akin to that of auto safety, is that of road design—the idea that better roads would also reduce the likelihood of accidents. Although these alternative frames are well known among policy experts, they have received little attention outside the expert research community and are not widely known among the general public.

More recently, a 'public health' frame has been advanced, implicating alcohol producers and distributors as major contributors to the problem of driving under the influence (DUI). In this frame, the alcohol industry is cast as the villain pursuing profits at the expense of public health. The essence of the frame is described by Gusfield (1988, p. 116-117) as follows: "From the perspective of an interest in public health, DUI is a facet of the problems produced by beverage alcohol. The countermeasures associated with the consumption and distribution of alcohol are central in this concern.... It is just as logical to control the institutions that sell alcohol, to treat chronic alcoholics or 'alcohol abusers,' and to maintain high prices on alcohol as it is to prohibit and punish DUI as a way of promoting automobile safety." In the same way tobacco companies are portrayed as attempting to hook young smokers to perpetuate the market for their product, alcohol producers are seen as targeting young people to create a lifelong clientele of heavy drinkers (McCarthy 1994).

The 'auto safety' and 'public health' frames both have their emotive aspects. Each has been advanced by a more or less organized group of advocates and each has achieved a wide degree of public acceptance (McCarthy 1994). The most popularly accessible versions of these frames possess dramatic attributes that personify big industry alcohol and automobile manufacturers as villain; "...a possible drama of scene, of environment, is converted into one of agent..." (Gusfield 1981, p. 82). Despite their dramatic and practical attributes, however, neither has had the emotional impact of the drunken driver and the conflict around them has generated almost none of the grass-roots involvement derived from the drunk driving frame. McCarthy (1994) notes the main dimensions of the frame were well in place by the time the citizens' movement against drunk driving emerged in the late 1970's. Here Gusfield (1981, p. 82) describes it main elements: "...the drinking driver is portrayed as 'drunk'...a permanent attribute of the person. Not the event 'drinking driving' but the person 'drunken driver' is described. The personalization of the event keeps alive the sense of a drama of conflict against disordered persons, a performance of deviance. It is a drama of agents in which the individual is prime mover." For those adopting the frame, the clear focus on personal responsibility makes detection and punishment of drunk drivers the obvious solution to the problem.

Emotive language, reviling the 'killer drunk' and battlefield imagery, as in the theme of 'waging war against drunk driving,' became increasingly more common just as the effective deterrence of drunk driving has come increasingly to rest on stiffer punishment of offenders (McCarthy 1994). With the rapid diffusion of a frame putting blame on the drunk driver, assessing potential means for remedying the problem became heavily weighted toward law enforcement approaches. Despite its original mandate to put auto safety reform on the national agenda, during the 1970's the NHTSA became the major institutional advocate of the drunk driving frame. Broad institutional and professional support was established and budgetary commitment expanded in accordance with the new frame's objectives. McCarthy (1994, p.140-141) found that: "Support was particularly strong among state and local functionaries, state and local police, and an expanding research community. All three of these groups had a stake in disseminating and institutionalizing the new frame; this was most true for local law enforcement officials.... Rates of arrest for DUI/DWI (driving under the influence/driving while intoxicated)...more than doubled during the 1970s across the United States, importantly as a result of these and other efforts of NHTSA.... From the beginning, NHTSA supported research efforts related to its concerns."

To summarize, professional and industrial interests played a significant role in creating and promoting the drunk driving frame in the U.S. Each of the frames examined makes very different 'sense' of similar 'facts.' With respect to cannabis and driving, statements issued by the former American 'drug czar' General Barry McCaffery support the idea that rhetorical framing is largely independent of the facts. For example, one reported finding that seven percent of fatal car crash victims tested positive for cannabis, compared to fifty-two percent for alcohol (NHTSA 1999), prompted McCaffery to proclaim that marijuana use is the number two cause of fatal car crashes in America. Considering that cannabis is detectable in the bloodstream up to a month or more after it is smoked, and that these concentrations tell us nothing about a driver's level of impairment (Robbe 1997), the percentage of fatalities that may be attributed to cannabis impairment exclusively is probably much lower than reported. And, based on previous estimates that put North American use rates at roughly ten percent of the general population (e.g., Boyd 1991), if ten percent of drivers use it once a month or more, the rate of cannabis related fatalities expected should exceed seven percent.

Are drivers who use cannabis really less likely than non-users to be involved in a fatal car accident? The question is reasonable in light of the evidence, and according to the data one might conclude that harm reduction efforts would be better invested elsewhere. Such notions are heretical for status quo supporters, for whom, as Gusfield (1981, p. 82) notes with drinking, the same facts and figures "...add up to a drama of morality and order in the explanation of auto accidents and deaths...dramatization creates a situation that predetermines the hypothesis" (Gusfield 1981, p. 82). From a prohibitionist understanding of the problem, General McCaffery's proclamation is logical and valid. After all, while drinking and driving is most certainly

80

wrong, using cannabis is wrong in itself. Moreover, it is a cause of vehicular carnage second only to alcohol consumption. Although the 'temperance mentality' has shifted over time, it continues to dominate North American drug policy.

The following discussion takes a closer look at often neglected underlying ideological dimensions and rhetorical shortcomings of the harm reduction movement. First we examine problems stemming from its compromise of principles, from the perspective of observers on different sides of the debate. From a drug reform perspective, harm reduction's one-sided focus contradicts its call for more 'cost-benefit' assessments. Ongoing concessions to the temperance mentality—as illustrated by successful efforts of opponents to quash a past proposal to relax the current laws—continue to define the cannabis controversy in terms largely dictated by endangerment themes. The rational discourse of harm reduction, I will argue, has done little to redress this imbalance, and may unwittingly contribute to reinforcing the predominant western temperance tradition.

## Philosophical Problems

Some of the issues at stake in the adoption and diffusion of harm reduction policies in the drugs arena—as in whether, for example, providing free needles to heroin users increases the rate of progression to injecting use—may eventually be resolved by empirical testing. Some of the more covert issues, however, are likely to remain a matter of philosophical dispute, the resolution of which will owe more to the power of advocates than the scientific veracity of their arguments (Hawks 1993). Later I examine the rhetorical implications and advantages of approaching drug reform from a human rights perspective. More immediately, my aim is to identify important philosophical considerations that may limit harm reduction's adoption in North America and elsewhere.

Reflecting on impediments to the global adoption of harm reduction policies, Hawks (1993, p. 94-95) points to the loss of idealism and fear of collusion with drug use such adoption implies. He argues: "To accept a need for harm reduction is, at least superficially, to give up on harm elimination—it is to accept the inevitability of harm, however desirable its minimisation. Although, when carried to its ultimate conclusion, harm reduction may amount to harm elimination, if one has subscribed to the belief that society can be rid of such harm, to collude with its minimisation is bound to seem like a compromise.... Afterall, if we talk of minimisation rather than elimination we clearly accept the inevitability, perhaps even the desirability, of

81

continued drug use."

To remove the idealism that argues life should be lived without recourse to drugs, or at least the illicit drugs, is to invite more drug use. Those who indulge in such reckless and deviant risk taking behaviour must accept the harmful consequences of their behaviour. From the above standpoint, assisting people to reduce the dangers of drug use only reinforces undesirable conduct. An entirely different impediment to the adoption of harm reduction principles is the growing distrust of governmental paternalism in our society (Hawks 1993). From a liberal perspective, much public health is overly paternalistic. Many of the measures invoked in harm reduction approaches to drug use require excessive regulation and unnecessary state intervention.

The central tenets of liberalism will be examined in more detail. For present purposes, I emphasize that whereas all libertarians are more or less committed to the veracity of the free market place, believing the market will behave in ways that maximize benefits to the whole of society, their levels of support for state intervention widely vary. For "conservative libertarians" (see Mitchell 1990; Szasz 1992), who uphold the sanctity of individual property and freedom of contract above all other principles, governmental controls on the drug market are strictly unacceptable no matter what the consequences. Less committed libertarians acknowledge modest government controls may be necessary to mitigate the inevitable free market abuses. "Civil libertarians" in particular tend to regard the freedom of contract with less deference than the right to privacy. They are more likely to argue around the right to use drugs. "And they are far more likely to integrate considerations of social justice and public health into their principles and policy calculations" (Nadelmann 1993, p. 40).

In contrast to abstinence oriented prohibitionism, with its roots in law enforcement and medical and religious paternalism, the harm reduction perspective is principally rooted in humanitarian and modern liberal philosophy (Cohen 1993). It has been noted, however, that harm reduction approaches tend to rely upon a utilitarian calculus of costs and benefits that fails to fully countenance the implications of a "supply/demand" approach to drug use. According to Hawks (1993, p. 95-96, italics in original), whereas supply interdiction will always be a component of any successful harm reduction campaign, attempts to prevent supply in the face of widespread demand for drugs can never be wholly successful. He argues: "Addressing the demand for drugs will mean acknowledging that drugs are used for a variety of purposes, not always out of an ignorance as to their effects or as an expression of 'pathologies' in the user.... Addressing the demand for drugs as one aspect of a supply/demand approach to the minimisation of drug-related harm will mean addressing the

82

complexity and the profundity of the issues raised by the question 'Why do people use drugs?'.... In many instances drugs are taken, not because people do not know what their effects will be, *but precisely because they do.*"

Although heavy drug users represent disproportionate levels of harm, the more moderate recreational users represent the bulk of harm simply because there are so many more of them (Mugford 1993). Thus, while harm reduction strategies that uphold the aggregate good over the rights of individuals to choose to use a drug safely seem counterintuitive in individualist cultures, without serious consideration of drug use having benefits, prohibition is a nonetheless rational alternative when looked from the perspective of utilitarianism. As noted previously, excitement and pleasure are not benefits that are easily defended from a harm reduction standpoint. Mugford (1993, p. 28) argues, "...unless one can defend pleasure and with it moments of non-rational hedonistic risk-taking (and possibilities of irresponsibility), any cost-benefit analysis of drug use will inevitably drift towards the evaluation of costs alone. In the case of illicit drugs, such a position necessarily drifts towards anti-drug, even prohibitionist sentiments."

In the following excerpt from my interview with Canadian psychologist Bruce Alexander, he also emphasizes certain problems with adopting a one-sided focus on harm. Attributing the deficits of harm reduction partly to the cultural implications of our temperance tradition, he stated: "...part of my frustration with it is that my friends are all with the harm reduction people in saying, 'Well it doesn't do too much harm, and you can control the harm it does.' And I want to say, 'What about the benefits?' Let's talk about that. Because the whole idea of doing a cost-benefit analysis without ever looking at the benefits is, to me, totally silly. And yet people just don't want to talk about it, and I'm not clear why because we all know if you're going to analyze anything meaningfully, you've got to talk about costs and benefits. That would be a normal economic way that we think, but people generally speaking won't do that, except very privately. It goes right back to the temperance movement."

"...from the start of the temperance movement, around 1830 let's say, they made it absolutely prohibited to talk about the benefits of alcohol. You could only talk about the harm...that's one of the straightjackets that we work within, and it's academics as well as other people who work within that straightjacket. I can't see why, but they do...it's all in the temperance literature. This is just one aspect of it too—the fact that you cannot talk about benefits, only costs. So I'm quite ambivalent about harm reduction. Harm reduction is saying we have all these costs and we can reduce, but that's only half an analysis, and

83

therefore I think it is still trapped within the temperance mentality. I think it's a concession to something else, and what the something else is is not as clear to me...probably there's a certain stage in capitalist development in which it really becomes important that the workers show up on Monday morning and not be drunk, and that people be clear-headed in a way so that they can watch those computer screens and this and that.... So I think it's a larger thing than just a Western thing."

[Isn't temperance more about moderation than prohibition?] "No, it's all about prohibition. Temperance is just a misnomer for it; they called it temperance, but it could have been called prohibitionism. The way it got that misnomer is that when they started around the 1800's, the initial temperance people really were in favour of moderational temperance. But very quickly, very very early on, by 1830 they were all about prohibition...." [Are we seeing changes in the temperance mentality over time?] "I don't know...what I think is that the temperance movement has changed its content. Originally it was an anti-alcohol movement, of course.... But in the modern form it's really saying, 'Well you know, alcohol is okay, but there are still devil drugs and they just happen to be something different.' So there's been that shift, and we may soon see marijuana shifted over to the side which is okay too. But still the essential concept of the temperance movement is that there are two classes of drugs, the demonic ones and the beneficial, wonderful ones.... That's the essential concept and that concept is as alive today as it ever was. It's just that the drugs on both sides have shifted, and it is I think a product or characteristic of culture that it demonizes."

"...if you go back in Western culture a few hundred years, you find the heretics who should be burned and whipped...and nothing good can be said about heresy. It's only bad, and I think that in some sense culture itself demonizes. It makes these kinds of divisions and it's quite cruel to the people on this left hand, and I think that we have simply pharmacologized that tendency.... It's a battle for the soul I think, and that battle for the soul is as much a part of our culture as any other. Because the culture depends upon winning the souls of a great mass of people and it must persecute those whose soul it has not won, and I think it's that kind of thing we're looking at. I mean the health issues are totally bogus. I don't think anybody can take them seriously if they look at them. That's not the issue—it's a loyalty issue." [So despite all that's written about rational reform, we must continue to work to make small differences within the same basic framework?] "Exactly, and I think it needs to be understood in this larger way, because I don't think we can do much about it.... It's an authoritarianism which grows out of a sort of natural defensive qualities of a culture. It does defend itself, and in a way maybe it has to. Maybe cultures must defend themselves."

Alexander's contention that prohibition may be a natural defensive mechanism serving to protect a culture from feared outside entities is consistent with Fromberg's (1993) organic metaphor of contagion likening prohibition to an allergic, or "socio-immunological," reaction in which society attacks harmless intruders, initiating a war against itself in the process. For Fromberg, prohibition is not an end in itself but rather a necessary stage of evolution in the acculturation of foreign drugs into the mainstream society. Citing the Dutch cannabis experience as an example, he argues the reaction to drugs starts as a 'normal' social disapproval and prohibition against a foreign invader and then, with increasing realization that prohibition cannot succeed, leads to policies to reduce harm. Whereas in Dutch law, however, legal sanctions are applied not as an end but as a means of social control, prohibition in more legalistic societies is enforced as a matter of principle. Effectiveness is irrelevant; the foreign agent, even if innocuous, must be attacked—even if the drugs we fight are harmless compared to other drugs, such as tobacco and alcohol, whose uses we accept.

As compared to the Dutch situation where cannabis has been gradually acculturated, or normalized, with the norms regulating use increasingly derived from mainstream social values, North American prohibitionism shows the kind of defensive over-reaction, provoking "secondary deviance and other inflammatory symptoms," that are typical of an allergic response (Fromberg 1993). With the gradual desensitization and normalization of cannabis in Holland, the user group has become less marginalized enabling mainstream social developments to promote harm reducing patterns of regulation and use. Harm reduction is promoted as a government protected matter of entitlement. In the Canadian context prohibition precludes these measures, stigmatizing substance use to the extent that even users tend to accept the dominant endangerment themes of a temperance society. Notwithstanding the compelling level of optimism engendered in an evolutionary understanding of the problem, whereby illicit drug use may gradually be normalized by way of societal acculturation and eventually rational reform, drug policy changes in Canada are still far from inevitable.

Considering the proliferation of cannabis use among otherwise conventional Canadians, one might indeed argue that societal diffusion and normalization of the drug inevitably will lead to confrontations over drug laws and eventual drug policy reform. However, with respect to a 'generational effect' prompting called for changes to the marijuana laws, longtime drug policy researcher Patricia Erickson contended: "First of all, cannabis isn't a drug that people are all that committed to; it's sort of take it or leave it. And if they grow up and decide it's not worth the risks, you don't have the same commitment that you might if you were a serious cocaine or heroin user. So I think that part of it's diluted, and part of it is when you have kids yourself you're always more circumspect. You're maybe not so sure that you want them using marijuana at thirteen or fourteen or fifteen. And the interviews I did with the adult long term users showed that most of them weren't for legalization. A minority were but a lot of them seemed to think that the same laws that had not deterred them were somehow going to have some effect on youth. I mean it's not very logical but there you have it, and I think it says something about the symbolic power of these norms against use."

"Bruce Alexander's right too; we're fundamentally a temperance oriented society and we fear the loss of control that drugs bring. So we fear it for our children and we fear it for others, and that can coexist with a view that we were perfectly able to control our drug use and that they weren't causing problems. We're not really willing to extend that to others.... It's hard really to understand, but it's there and I don't know what would change it exactly and fundamentally. It's maybe not that reachable by rational analysis or empirical data...you have to realize that 25 years ago I thought my job would be over in a couple of years as far as marijuana research, because I really was so sure the law would change after the LeDain Commission, and I can't be anything but a cynic after 25 years and the accumulation of data. Canada has some of the best data anywhere in the world about drug producing effects and the harms of the law. And there's a lot of us that have done the critique part and yet we've had this new law come into place which is even worse than the old law..."

"There is this fundamental reluctance to say that we would accept cannabis as a recreational drug in society. That's still a long way from being resolved.... And there is the question of youth. And we still try to argue around harm reduction that actually allowing adult use of cannabis and making it normal to use in a controlled way, and appreciating the effects honestly and objectively, is more likely to decrease adolescent use than increase it, because you then draw a line like you do with alcohol. It doesn't mean that there wouldn't be experimentation, but you haven't kind of targeted it as much for adolescents as something that they can do that the adults are so hypocritical about. But that's still a pretty hard argument to make, and I don't think that it's generally acceptable at this point among so-called adolescent specialists and drug educators in the traditional way."

Whereas traditional approaches to drug education and treatment tend towards a "mechanistic view" of drug use and addiction founded on the "worst case scenario" in which passive users become compulsive users and persist despite the consequent harms to themselves and others, Erickson (1993) favours a "volunteeristic" approach wherein the user is capable of weighing benefits and risks to make responsible decisions about consumption. Noting the ineffectiveness of formal controls to curtail drug use, she argues a shift from the prevailing mechanistic view to a volunteeristic approach is required in order to build a risk-reducing drug subculture built on informal means of control. By countering public understanding of responsible, regulated use by otherwise conventional people, the traditional anti-drug campaigns and 'drug education' featuring scare tactics that marginalize and misinform users would seem to do more harm than good.

A volunteeristic approach by comparison allows for greater flexibility in treatment to determine more practical goals than strict abstinence. Recognizing the majority of users do not want to be 'cured' of their drug use so much as continue to use without adverse consequence (Hawks 1993), such an approach would attract committed recreational users and educate others to the reality and potential for controlled drug use and harm reduction policy development. Education providing a balanced view of both risks and benefits could be used to encourage safer casual use and experimentation and still stop short of the active promotion of drug use (Erickson 1993). Nevertheless, as noted by Erickson above, this is still a hard argument to make among traditional drug educators. There still is a fundamental reluctance to accept even a 'soft drug' like cannabis as a recreational drug in our society.

At the root of endangerment claims as to the social and personal harms caused by cannabis and other prohibited drugs, the theme of moral depravity, whether explicit or otherwise, predominates prohibitionist rhetoric. Despite its scientific styling today, the prohibition argument is grounded in a long standing moral tradition that continues to dictate the context of public debate. The dangers of drug use are ordinarily taken for granted and require explication only when the assumptions upholding prohibition come under attack by reformers. The more alarmist type claims are most prevalent, as in the early period preceding drug prohibition in Canada, when the threat of public endangerment is perceived to be increasing. Accordingly, it is noteworthy that the more alarming prohibitionist claims I encountered in this study came in direct opposition to proposals aimed at relaxing criminal controls over cannabis.

Here I draw on testimonies from two status quo defenders to illustrate the vitriol and (mis)appropriation of science in support of temperance ideology. Testifying to the Standing Senate Committee on Legal and Constitutional Affairs, Charles Perkins—the Chairman of the Board of Directors of the Lambton Families in Action—opposed a proposition aimed at relaxing penalties for cannabis possession (Bill C-8, an ill-fated proposal that came prior to the enactment of the 1996 Controlled Drugs and Substances Act). As noted previously, the CDSA put cannabis in a separate category from cocaine and heroin, but its criminal status was maintained. Despite earlier talk of a decriminalization provision in the Act, the Senate Committee succeeded in passing a revamped version of the 1969 Narcotic Control Act (NCA) with no major changes (see Erickson 1998).

Stated Perkins: "Our biggest concern with Bill C-8 is with some of the parts which deal with cannabis and the lessening of laws regarding possession. For the purposes of this presentation, it does not matter whether cannabis is called hemp, marihuana, hashish or hash oil—they all come from the same plant and they are all drugs.... Cannabis has absolutely no redeeming social value. Any use of cannabis is abuse. People use it for no other reason than to get stoned out of their minds. The myth about cannabis being a 'soft drug' must be dispelled. What is so soft about a drug that is a catalyst for violent behaviour, which triggers schizophrenia and marihuana psychosis, is fetal toxic and mutagenic and, as such, can have a negative impact on the physical and mental well-being of the unborn? Many children in this country have been born with deficiencies as a result of parental cannabis consumption. These children are the innocent victims of someone else's cannabis use. Cannabis compromises the immune system, is more carcinogenic than tobacco, has an addiction rate three to seven times greater than alcohol, breaks down the genetic code in males and, in females, either injures or destroys the eggs in the ovaries. Cannabis slows down the function of the brain and makes a person unable to fulfill the demands of a high-tech information society. Cannabis causes impairment that can last for over 24 hours. The list goes on. Is this what a 'soft drug' is supposed to do? We are not talking about pancake batter here."

"If people would pay more attention to the findings of the scientific community and less to the philosophical community, they would be well aware that cannabis is the most misunderstood, the most invasive and the most dangerous drug available on our streets. We cannot allow probable conjecture and philosophical speculation to take precedence over scientific fact. Since 1979, there have been over 12,000 documented scientific studies done on cannabis. Not one of those studies has proven cannabis safe or effective for anything. If anyone tries to tell you differently, they are not being upfront and honest with you. When anyone suggests removing the criminality from cannabis, the question that they cannot answer is: Why would any society want to create and finance a system that leads to nothing but sickness and dependence? In Canada right now it is almost impossible for any adolescent to receive in-service treatment for drug addiction, be it cannabis or any other drug. The only sure way to receive treatment is to be convicted and incarcerated for some other crime. Of particular concern is this 30-gram nonsense in the bill.... What this 30-gram business

88

tells the youth of your country is, 'It is all right to smoke dope, as long as you have less than 30 grams or 100 joints on you at any one time.' User-dealers will have a field day with this law as it establishes a benchmark for how much cannabis a person can have without being charged for trafficking."

"The wide variance in the THC levels which is anywhere from 1 per cent to over 30 per cent in this country makes this approach very dangerous. Hypothermia is a very real risk when people smoke cannabis with high levels of THC. In the minds of our youth, diminishing the consequences of possession of cannabis also reduces the perception of risk. We have seen what a horrendous failure the 30-gram approach to cannabis has been for the youth of the Netherlands. Why do we want to inflict some other country's failure on Canadians, especially our youth? After over a decade of a reduction in adolescent drug use, there has been a reversal in that trend. Since the reintroduction of the 'failed' responsible use messages of the 1970s—this is now called 'harm reduction'—and the media's obsession with beating the drum for decriminalization and/or legalization, adolescent drug use is now back up to where it was in 1980, which just happened to be the last time legislation was presented to soften our laws concerning cannabis."

"Our youth are Canada's most valuable natural resource. We cannot afford to jeopardize the mental and physical well-being of this resource because of a perception about a drug. The softening of any of our drug laws serves no useful purpose.... For the sake of Canada's youth, it is of the utmost importance that you not pass Bill C-8 or any other bill that promotes drug use by softening the laws, be it cannabis or any other drug. In closing, I offer you this excerpt from a statement made by the Central Narcotics Intelligence Bureau of the Egyptian government in one of its annual reports. It states: 'the prepared product of the cannabis sativa plant...is capable of profoundly disturbing the brain cells and of inducing acts of violence, even murder. It is in fact a thoroughly vicious and dangerous thing of no value whatever to humanity and deserving of nothing but the odium and contempt of civilized people.' That statement was made in 1944. Scientific research has proven time and time again how very true that statement was and still is."

Stating he concurred with Mr. Perkins testimony about the seriousness of cannabis consumption by young people, Fred Burford, President of the Council on Drug Abuse (CODA), went on to introduce several other 'facts' which I have summarized for the sake of brevity below. Mr. Burford remarked that: "...We have wonderful youth in Canada. They care deeply for others and have a highly developed social conscience. Canadian decision-makers and influencers have the responsibility to foster an environment in which youth can have the best opportunity to reach their potential. Also the safety and health of youth should be prime concerns. I am representing CODA here today for the sake of our country's kids. The main controversy regarding Bill C-8 seems to swirl around the status of cannabis under the bill. Keeping youth in mind, the three main adverse effects of cannabis that are conclusive are the following. There are many, and Charles Perkins has listed many, but there are three that are conclusively agreed upon by the experts: First, short-term memory and cognitive learning; second, affects on coordination, judgment, perception of time and space, and speed of reaction; and, third, the respiratory system. It is very important to note that the percentage of THC in marihuana was seven times greater in 1994 than it was in 1975. I repeat: Seven times greater... The truth about cannabis is starting to emerge."

"As to the effects on coordination and judgment...for vehicle crashes, 10 to 15 per cent of them are mainly due to marihuana impairment. What a startling development! Of all the vehicle crashes, it is not alcohol being the main cause exclusively now but 10 to 15 per cent because of marihuana. That represents a large number of tragedies...a hangover effect, muscle incoordination, and drowsiness may last after the "high" has passed, making it risky to drive or engage in other potentially dangerous tasks for at least several hours—even if the user believes that he or she has recovered completely. I can guarantee that there are very few of our youth who are aware of this effect...teenage marihuana use results in diminished academic performance for far too many using students and, consequently, these students do not reach their potential. These are human tragedies. As to coordination problems, marihuana use increases unnecessary injuries and deaths because of its adverse affects on the user's coordination, etcetera. Safety in schools is in jeopardy, in gyms, labs, shops, swimming pools, vehicles on and off school property. The 'hangover effect' that I referred to increases this safety problem. With regard to health, we have to treat very seriously any drug that weakens and causes problems to the respiratory systems of youth."

"In summary, it is obvious that out of concern for the health, safety and futures of youth, no change in the cannabis law should be made that could result in a major increase in teenage use of cannabis...if amendments to Bill C-8 were brought in such that youth viewed the consequences as trivial and tantamount to removing the legal restrictions on cannabis, then this would be a major change. An example of this kind of change would be a traffic-ticket type summons approach.... The traffic ticket type summons makes no sense from an epidemiological standpoint nor is it consistent with the function of the criminal law in Canada. Berman of Harvard and the late Professor Desmond Morton stress the uses of the law as a social institution. Part of its function is to control, as Berman says, tendencies and acts 'which we may never really master ourselves.' In other words, the use of the law for its denunciation of a behaviour is important as a declaration of things we as a society do not condone. A traffic ticket summons does not make such a declaration" (Standing Senate Committee on Legal and Constitutional Affairs: Ottawa, April 24, 1996).

Of some related interest, three years later, in the Spring of 1999, the national association of police chiefs and the Royal Canadian Mounted Police both came out in support of decriminalizing cannabis possession. The explanation was that decriminalization would conserve limited drug enforcement resources by making the option of a traffic-ticket type summons available to police. But with regard to Burford's claims, which are questionable of course (moreover, such extreme beliefs about the dangers of cannabis are probably not shared by every status quo defender)—their factual basis is of little relevance here. More important presently than their scientific accuracy are what they represent in terms of differing opinion and essential conflicts at the core of these debates. As long as legal institutions continue to define the use of marijuana as a crime aimed at protecting Canadians from an act "we may never master ourselves," more pragmatic and enlightened orientations are untenable.

At the core of the debates over cannabis reform lies the fundamental dispute over the balance of power between drugs and the human will. The drug control debate, like other disputes over justice in the public realm, is a matter not for rational enquiry but for the assertion and counterassertion of incompatible sets of premises (MacIntyre 1988). Attention to the rhetoric of social problems claims making is critical to understanding harm, justice, even rationality itself, as "essentially contested concepts" (Gallie 1962) that are not amenable to rational standards and solutions. Scientific arguments which deny their own rhetoric are severely disadvantaged in policy disputes over the definition of values and their application. In moral debates factual evidence is seldom decisive (Czubaroff 1989). By emphasizing a one-sided focus on harm that excludes possible benefits of drug use, harm reduction's underlying moral foundation has been sacrificed in exchange for an illusion of neutral standing that is rarely respected outside academic circles.

'Solving' a moral problem is not like a skill that can be judged against professional standards of rationality. Such problems are only problems in the sense that they will continue to be argued between and within opposing traditions of discourse, not because they are necessarily resolvable. Arguing for social change requires that we make a choice between rival "traditions of argumentation" (Shotter 1993) that can only be judged and justified in a particular context of local circumstances. If one is rooted in those circumstances and has grounds for that choice, there is always a 'best' choice we can justify to others. Since

91

policy reform opponents carry the authority of established belief, or "presumption" (Czubaroff 1989), conceptual innovation by way of pragmatic reform requires moral grounding in a tradition providing the necessary resources for critical inquiry.

The parable of Buridan's Ass (Signorile 1989) is instructive. When faced with two equally attractive piles of hay, the indecisive mule starved to death for want of a logical preference. Strict rationality is irrational because it is immobilizing. The impetus for action always comes from outside the system. For those seeking to make rationality relevant and take a more active role in public policy debates, harm reductionists, indeed all social scientists, are well advised to examine more closely the moral foundations of their work. Returning to Best's (1987) earlier dichotomy of rhetoric in claims making, the abandonment of moral warrants in favour of strictly rational arguments is limiting in light of these contentions. While he stresses that most claims incorporate both moral and rational themes, Best (1987, p. 116) contends experienced claims makers operating in well-established social movements—working from a "...beachhead of accepted principles established during earlier campaigns for reinterpretation"—tend to favour a rhetoric of rationality.

As part of an established social movement firmly grounded in the public health perspective, harm reduction is imminently well-suited for revealing the logical flaws in prohibition by way of empirical analysis. Such later stage social problems campaigns "...tend to feature more detailed agendas for policy changes, as well as a clearer sense of which items—whether out of principle or pragmatism—deserve priority" (Best 1987, pp. 116-117). The established "beachhead of accepted principles," or moral warrants behind the movement to which it might profitably lay claim, are the very principles that have yet to be established by harm reduction policy supporters. The greatest challenge for harm reduction lies in the promotion of its underlying ideals. By glossing over these ideals (chief among them quite simply that "drug users are people too") to try and claim a middle-ground position (Nadelmann 1993), harm reduction undermines its inherent humanism in the process, sacrificing the respect for individual free will and human adaptive potential that is at the core of the tradition.

Preferring to keep such ideological, liberty based values out of the analysis, harm reduction opts for a morally neutral form of inquiry wherein respect for human rights is exchanged for a utilitarian calculus in which individual autonomy and rights have no moral value in and of themselves. Harm reduction style rhetoric, with its illusion of neutral standing in the name of empirical reason, is strategically flawed insofar as it disavows the moral footing that is needed to address prohibitionism as both an immoral and irrational approach to drug policy. While noting there are certain political advantages, I have focused on rhetorical shortcomings of this strategy. And I have argued harm reduction stands to benefit from greater emphasis on values and morality, thus laying claim to a well-established tradition of argumentation with the necessary rhetorical resources for advancement.

Insofar as harm reduction favours rational analysis and education over more repressive approaches to drug use, it is largely reflective of the liberal tradition with its broader critique of government intrusions in the private domain, particularly the prohibition of acts involving non-violent crimes without victims. In the next chapter, modern liberalism is conceptually delineated as a morally coherent and viable foundation from which to argue the case for drug law reform. Despite the North American fashion of denigrating its adherents and consequent muddling of the idea, the concept of 'liberalism' is herein presented as *the* moral tradition of modern Western culture and thereby the most defensible rhetorical standpoint for countering the injustice of marijuana prohibition.

## Summary

This chapter began with a discussion of the practical and political problems that hinder harm reduction as a drug reform strategy. Despite the evident advantages of achieving common ground between the prohibitionists and so-called legalizers, through a stance of moral and political neutrality, I have also noted there are certain disadvantages. Harm reduction, in particular, has been increasingly coopted by opposing forces whose emphasis is clearly on the side of prohibition and/or 'treating' substance users to their abstinence agenda. Although political neutrality would seem advantageous in the contemporary context of rational debate, it is a weakness insofar as it encourages cooption. The respect for human rights at the core of harm reduction is fundamentally negated by a one-sided focus on harm that precludes possible benefits. With reference to youth drug use and impaired driving, it was argued, that assessments of drug harm are more a matter of cultural values than empirical reasoning will allow.

Notwithstanding arguments for rational debate, the main disagreement between prohibitionists and reformers centres on the essentially contested balance of power between drugs and the human will. The deeply embedded moral tradition of temperance dominates discourse on drug use, shaping public understanding of the issues and responses in terms that ultimately favour a prohibitionist perspective. In moral debates, we have noted above that factual evidence is seldom conclusive. In this light, the primary challenge for harm reduction lies in promoting the respect for human rights at the root of the perspective. In so doing its proponents might lay claim to well-established moral warrants with evaluative weight that closely rivals those of their opponents. These arguments are developed in additional detail in chapter five with reference to the liberal tradition and strategies available under the *Charter of Rights and Freedoms*. In the legal-political context of Canadian drug policy, I conclude that factual assessments of drug harm and harm reduction are ancillary to advancing societal perceptions of drug use as a right deserving constitutional protection.

## CHAPTER FIVE
## FROM HARM REDUCTION TO HUMAN RIGHTS

Returning to Best's (1987) dichotomy of rhetoric in claims making, harm reduction is consistent with his general description of a later stage drug reform strategy. As a well-established multidisciplinary movement, harm reduction is promoted by a diverse range of experienced claims makers who invoke the rhetoric of rationality as a means to shape drug policy decision making. To reiterate Best's argument, whereas early stage social problem constructions are comprised of demands to acknowledge or adopt a new orientation to the problem, and tend to be directed at an already converted or openly hostile audience, later campaigns feature more detailed agendas for change and a clearer sense of implementation priorities. Whereas inexperienced claims makers in germinal social movements must attract media attention and appeal to 'the people' with straightforward moral themes commonly propelled by outrage, experienced claims makers operating inside political circles see their audience as persuadable by way of rational arguments. Later stage social problems campaigns tend to favour a rhetoric of rationality, following up earlier established moral warrants for change with a concrete plan of action designed to shape policy.

As noted previously, however, such a simplistic dichotomy hardly does justice to the complexity of claims making, as rhetorical work inevitably involves choosing to emphasize the claims deemed most persuasive in light of their cultural context and audience. A strategic conception of social problems claims making acknowledges a range of rhetorical choices, recognizing that most claims will incorporate both moral and rational themes. The foregoing analysis of harm reduction rhetoric suggests that Best's dichotomy requires some modification. Most importantly, on examining discursive limitations, it has been argued harm reduction lacks the moral foundation needed to effectively manoeuvre as a later stage social problems campaign. As a self-styled morally neutral approach to the drug problem, disregarding any appeal to moral

95

warrants for change, harm reduction is better understood as an adaptive rhetorical stage in a developing drug reform movement. In the contemporary context of global prohibition, rather than an ultimate rational end or solution, harm reduction may be more of a stepping stone strategy towards a thematically integrated moral-rational approach to the drug problem.

Accordingly our focus shifts away from emphasizing the rational standards of empirical science towards the legal-political arenas and means by which moral problems are more fruitfully contested. In this chapter we examine the cannabis reform issue with an eye to developing the human rights perspective and arguments available under constitutional democracy. Advancing the drugs debate in Canada may inevitably owe more to the legal interpretation and protection of rights embodied in constitutional arrangements than to the empirical perfection of a harm reduction science. Although the latter has a prominent role in developing pragmatic alternatives to prohibition policy, it is nevertheless needful of a rhetorical foundation by which to denounce prohibition as a morally objectionable intervention in the private lives of individuals. While avowedly liberal drug reform strategies may seem boldly out of step with current policy debates, a human rights view of drug use is as ideologically viable in western culture as our ongoing concessions to the prohibitionist mentality. Before elaborating further in this chapter, harm reduction is described in the next section as a stepping stone toward a human rights approach to substance use.

## Harm Reduction as a Stepping Stone Strategy

Despite its ideological limitations, harm reduction is a logical counter-development to pro-prohibition arguments presented as good science. Abdicating moral warrants for change in the name of strictly rational solutions, harm reduction rhetoric may be a necessary stepping stone to broader reform where more confrontational challenges to the dominant order are perceived as too politically volatile. Harm reduction is a sympathetic or "tactical" (Ibarra and Kitsuse 1993) form of criticism, a counterrhetorical strategy that accepts in part the problematic status of conditions, but not suggested remedies for solving the 'drug problem.' Such an approach exemplifies the 'insider' political style of the liberal, as opposed to radical, reformer who is willing to discuss tactics and work with the system to initiate change. As a tactical concession to the prohibitionist mentality, harm reduction is generally sympathetic to the dominant theme of endangerment, making room for the more conventional understanding that most people do not take drugs and do not like the idea that other people do.

Whereas under prohibition a more liberal conception of *tolerance*—liberal in the sense of being disinclined to interfere with others' ways of living or opinions—may not extend to drug use, the practice may be nevertheless *tolerated* (that is, put up with or endured) as a matter of absolute necessity. The idea that harm reduction is more of a stepping stone strategy than a long term solution to the drug problem was first raised in my interview with Dr. Diane Riley. After decrying the lack of official acceptance and funding for harm reduction among the signatory countries of the United Nations, Riley turned to address human rights violations inflicted on drug users all over the world. In view of current global political realities, and the corresponding rhetorical strengths of harm reduction, she notes that there are certain limitations to pursuing a human rights approach to drug reform. Following up on her remarks about the stance of UN, I asked: "Is more ground being made on the human rights side of drug use than in harm reduction?"

Dr. Riley replied: "No, there's very little ground being made on the human rights side of it, because people really just pay lip service to the human rights side of it. Some countries have managed to get some legislative change on the basis of human rights or personal rights and so on, but mostly the changes have been around harm reduction as a health measure. Even though I would never define harm reduction without it including human rights changes, in many countries what you really have to play up to sell it is the health side of it and cost effectiveness side of it. Because in most countries, trying to sell anything on a human rights platform is useless. Especially, that's true in places like Malaysia. Well you know, forget it; you have to find some other way in there." [So despite your earlier comments on the overall lack of acceptance for harm reduction principles, it's still the best prospect for changes in policy?]

"Well yes, because most places are just paying lip service to it, including Canada. I mean we have a little bit of needle exchange and it's done badly and you end up getting problems with rates soaring and so on, because it's just like dabbling with harm reduction—not adopting it seriously, not adopting it comprehensively. And I think you've got a lot of that going on in a number of places. I think it's the answer and it's a stepping stone towards broader policy reform. The end's got to be much more than harm reduction, but it's a good stepping stone, and for the moment I think it's the solution to many problems. It's a way of staving off what we can't stave off.... I think it'll get worse before it gets better. And it's in that getting worse that we may be able to work out a way of things getting better...a lot of it will happen at the community level out of desperation. And we've seen tremendous changes in Asia and India and even China. I would think because of the need, the necessity for harm reduction, it would just become the movement to save what they

97

can save."

In the international context of global prohibition, particularly in nations lacking the necessary basis and procedures for appeal to human rights, Riley argues harm reduction has emerged as a practical public health solution grounded in necessity. Although she notes in many countries, including Canada, harm reduction has not been adopted seriously and is applied haphazardly at best, it is a good stepping stone to broader drug policy reform. While harm reduction has arisen out of sheer desperation in many third world nations, it is seldom adopted as a matter of principle. In North America, where the impending public health crisis is still largely unacknowledged, she contends the prohibitionist response to drugs may well intensify before there is official recognition of alternatives. Dr. Riley continues: "I think things will probably in the States, possibly even in Canada, become that much more rigid, and the UN will then try to impose that worldwide, that we'll see a clamping down period, even more so. That's what I think will happen anyway, but that all the while you've got now this massive international harm reduction movement as well as Amnesty's now becoming involved with these issue. So you're going to have the countermovement gaining force and eventually winning through, but I think in the next five to ten years there's going to be a real struggle over that..."

"I think it's only going to be through keeping up the international awareness, keeping alive the activism on it, that this is going to stand up. And that means that there's got to be funding to keep it going, and that's getting harder and harder to find, and there's got to be interest in it at all levels. And one of the things that's driven that interest has been AIDS. ...one of the only reasons we have harm reduction is because of AIDS. People wouldn't have really looked for drug policy change if it hadn't been for that. And if it hadn't been for the fact that AIDS potentially effects them and their children and their families, of course, they wouldn't give a damn about drug users or drug policy reform. And I think to the extent that we see a lessening interest in HIV in certain parts of the world...before we start to see more concern about Hepatitis C and D and E, F, and G, and all the other pathogens, there will be a period when there's a dropping off of concern before the realization that that was only the beginning, and there's all these other things we have to be aware of as well.... There's going to be this major right wing crackdown, which I'm sure is how it will start off, and then the other option of course is looking for more humane longer term solutions, which I think hopefully that's how it will start to evolve."

As a drug reform advocate and activist, Riley remains guardedly optimistic about the long term

98

prospects of the harm reduction movement and support for human rights of users. Despite making significant inroads in the public health community following the recent onslaught of AIDS and other fearsome epidemics, even well-established harm reduction initiatives, meeting with general indifference and often considerable opposition from moral conservatives, require continual struggle to survive. Whereas some limited changes in policy have proven permissible on practical grounds even to staunch prohibitionists, harm reduction fails to promote change as a matter of principle so it has been susceptible to cooption and negation. Insofar as the ongoing trials of the movement point to the hardened reality of global prohibition, we are reminded of the need to move slowly. We are also reminded of the rhetorical limitations of a rational perspective that lacks the moral capacity to address prohibition as a violation of the rights of substance users. While implementing harm reduction may be the immediate solution to public health crises, such as the threat of Hepatitis and HIV epidemics among intravenous drug users in particular, Dr. Riley remains hopeful that drug policies will evolve even further in the search for "more humane longer term solutions."

A similar concern for the goal of "humanizing" drug policy is stressed by legal scholar Robert Solomon below. In deriding the intransigence of North American drug policy, Solomon contends that the evidence supporting decriminalizing marijuana is overwhelming in terms of costs, benefits, and humanitarian principles alike. He is careful to emphasize, however, that there are ways we can humanize the drug laws short of actually decriminalizing. Short of decriminalizing marijuana, he argues that the law can be used in a way that is more consistent with the harm it presents in comparison to other offenses. For example: "...I see the virtues of moving away from criminalizing. You move away from criminalizing on the basis that it's causing more harm than good. You move away from criminalizing on principles of humanizing society.... I think the reasons are overwhelming both from a theoretical perspective and also from a humanitarian perspective, and a utilitarian perspective."

"I think the logical starting point to me is, because you can't start all over again and pretend we have no history...simply humanizing the drug laws. And how do you do that? Well, there's all kinds of things you can do short of decriminalizing...you could rein in police powers to be more consistent with the harm that is posed. The greater the risk in terms of safety, the greater the authority you're willing to give police. Duh! That's not harm minimization; it's common sense. This is using law in a way that most protects the most important values, which are life. So you could limit, you could get rid of, some of the draconian features of our law, and there are lots of them.... We could dramatically reduce all of the penalties, simply to make sure

99

that the penalty provisions reflect the seriousness of the offence...you can get rid of the possibility of jail for a first time offence. That doesn't involve decriminalizing; it is humanizing the law. And the last thing you could do is you could create a system to get rid of the adverse criminal record consequences of possession offenses."

"You could do all of that without decriminalizing. You would make the law less draconian, more humanitarian, more consistent with other laws in more keeping with the risk posed. None of that involves changing the legal status of marijuana.... Do I think it would make a huge difference if we moved from current criminal sanction to no criminal sanction for private possession? No. No, I don't think it would make much difference in terms of public harm. I don't think we'd have a lot to lose. I do have a sense that as long as we're next door to the United States, we'd have to move very, very slowly. There just is not going to be the political will.... So I don't think our society is ready to move that way in large part because people don't want the question."

"I don't want to question the two scotches I have when I come home before dinner and the Valium I take before I go to bed. I don't want to say if my kid misuses drugs, it's because he has seen me self-medicate; we're not going to go there.... And so our kids say, 'If you take the scotch, why shouldn't I smoke a joint?' It's a hard argument to answer.... So I tend to think we can make some considerable progress. Where I'd like to see us moving is to gradually demystify and undemonize illicit drugs. If we have to get there through first harm reduction, decriminalization, before we move to rational drug scheduling, so be it. But even the first stage of getting rid of the draconian features is still progress and if harm reduction is part of that, that's great." Once again harm reduction is described as a potential stepping stone towards humane application of our drug laws. While Professor Solomon is more ambivalent than Riley about the need for harm reduction as a distinctive drug reform strategy, their assessments are consistent as to the relative unimportance of achieving marijuana law reform.

Indeed it was a common theme in interviews that cannabis is a minor issue compared to other problems due to bad drug policies all around the world. According to Solomon, Canada may not have much to lose by decriminalizing marijuana, but it would probably make little difference in terms of actual harm. The potential benefits of moving toward legalization are far less compelling than they are in the U.S. He argues: "If Canada were to move to legalize drugs, we wouldn't get the same benefits because our drug trade isn't as associated with violence as theirs is. Our prisons aren't jammed at multi-billion dollars worth of drug prisoners." The foregoing conception of cannabis as being a minor drug policy issue in Canada would seem to limit the effectiveness of harm reduction arguments as a rhetorical strategy. This observation is extended in the following discussion of the common tendency to trivialize the issue as a potential barrier to marijuana law reform.

## The Triviality of Cannabis

Characterizing harm reduction as a stepping stone towards more humane drug policy is somewhat problematic with respect to marijuana laws. The cumulative evidence and common recognition of the harmlessness of cannabis compared to other drugs preclude it from becoming a political priority. The symbolic importance of the cannabis issue as a gateway to broader reform is regularly acknowledged, even fearfully by some among the ranks of status quo defenders. At the same time, its importance is easily trivialized in terms of the public health priorities of the harm reduction movement. As I noted previously, though cannabis is invariably the first drug proposed for reform during any discussion of drug policy—compared to heroin, cocaine, and other drugs that are generally agreed to be more harmful—it is seldom prominently discussed in the context of harm reduction (Morgan et al. 1993).

Notwithstanding the strong arguments for law reform assuming a rational analysis of the costs and benefits, as compared to other illicit and regulated substances with glaring public health implications, cannabis is apparently so innocuous as to attract little serious attention in the area of harm reduction. Considering her emphasis on the AIDS epidemic as a primary focus of drug policy reform, I asked Diane Riley to compare the two concerns: [Is the marijuana issue then only secondary to your concern with AIDS and other problems of intravenous drug use?] "Yes, it's just different. In the States certainly it's a major issue, because of the number of people that get locked up and the sentences and so on. But worldwide my concern is for just general policy reform, because marijuana is not the chief issue...the chief issues are around all drugs, and around HIV and Hepatitis C, and the violation of human rights of users—the lack of treatment, the lack of services, the appalling conditions, the use of prisons as 'treatment' facilities—all of those things."

"So marijuana is an interest because there needs to be reform, and there are far too many people who ·can get a criminal record even still, despite the wording of the new law. But no, compared to the harms worldwide, or even in Canada, there are many, many, many greater harms than marijuana. I mean if you look at the condition of our prisons and drug users in prisons and so on, it is not the chief concern.... I think it's going to be interesting over the next while and there's going to be a lot of changes, but I just think that it's

101

almost a distraction from the needs of the broader issues of drug policy reform." While cannabis reform may be supported by the movement, it is far from a harm reduction priority. Considering the more severe drug problems and violations of human rights alluded to by Riley, the movement to decriminalize marijuana in Canada seems trivial by comparison.

Furthermore, according to Morgan and his colleagues, even decriminalizing for medicinal purposes only is easily trivialized from a harm reduction standpoint, because it would invite inevitable comparisons between cannabis and the more widely accepted pharmaceutical alternatives that are already available under legal prescription (Morgan et al. 1993). The connection between medical marijuana and its wider acceptance for recreational purposes emerged as a noteworthy contention between respondents in this study. While the medical marijuana movement is expanding on the basis of its independence from the broader reform issue, and is largely outside the scope of our discussion, opinions on its relevance was found to vary widely. Though for some the two are wholly independent issues, other informants saw them as essentially inseparable. Still others, more equivocal, uncertain on the matter, were discovered to be somewhere in between.

In terms of biological harm and toxicity, cannabis compares favourably to many widely prescribed pharmaceuticals and is recognized as having many medical applications. However, tenuous support from the medical community has been offset considerably by warnings against smoked cannabis due to the risk of cardiopulmonary damage. Short of incontrovertible evidence to demonstrate its effectiveness compared to more conventional and easily regulated alternatives, unconditional support for the medical right to use cannabis is neither a natural nor necessary consequence of the harm reduction argument. Even drug reform advocates that remain uncommitted to harm reduction programming as a policy objective tend to downplay cannabis in terms of rational priorities. Although its low toxicity and health benefits were widely acknowledged by drug policy reformers, marijuana prohibition was seldom described as a major social policy concern.

This view is expounded in the following excerpt from my interview with Bruce Alexander. He argued: "...it's unusually benign compared to Prozac or Lithium or Thorazine. I mean, these are dangerous drugs and cannabis isn't.... So yeah, as drugs go, cannabis is quite a good drug and to give someone, for example, cannabis in treatment of schizophrenia is a wonderful advance. If the alternative is Thorazine or Prozac, you're really doing something for them if you can get them on cannabis instead.... I mean it needs to be recognized as a drug with some medical value. That can be overstated; that's the only reason I'm a little hesitant about it.... It's just another drug, but it's a good drug, it's a relatively safe drug, it's a drug which makes you feel nice. And some of the drugs don't make you feel nice. Well, I think we should use the ones that make us feel nice."

"...I think we think of it too much as a drug issue. I don't think drugs are that important. I mean, I like marijuana; it's a nice drug. But it's not that important...and to some extent, I sort of am dismayed to see so many bright young people wasting their time on dope as an issue. Not that it isn't an issue. It's a real issue, but it's an issue for our lifestyles. It's kind of nice; we could have a nicer life if those laws are relaxed. But they're already relaxed. Nothing much is going to change if the drug is actually legalized. It's already legalized for practical purposes. And there are important issues, and in that sense I have a little backlash in my own mind about both harm reduction and marijuana. Because I want to say, 'Well come on; there are real problems out there.'" Citing the relaxed social attitude and response towards marijuana in Canada—in relation to 'real social problems,' such as maintaining fish stocks and national autonomy in the face of US trade agreements, for example—Alexander finds it difficult to justify the time and energy that is being expended on the issue.

While it may be a safe drug which offers some advantages over many other kinds of drug use, the benefits, like harms of use, are often overstated. Moreover, he contends that with regard to harm reduction, the move toward *de facto* decriminalization in many places suggests the harms of prohibition are no longer such a problem. Cannabis reform is more an "issue for our lifestyles;" nothing much would actually change if it were legalized. Assuming widely loosened enforcement of the law, claims of extensive harm from prohibition, for Alexander, should not be taken too seriously. This theme underlying several statements I recorded suggests substantial barriers to law reform may be attributed as much to the triviality of cannabis as to the more familiar allegations of drug harm. This contention is developed later on through illustration of the separation between factual and constitutional assessments of the cannabis debate. As a counterpoint to tendencies to trivialize the issue, however, first I will return to the matter of advancing the argument for human rights.

Here it is important to reiterate that despite widespread social tolerance and the use of police discretion to mitigate the adverse consequences of bad drug laws, as long as cannabis possession remains a criminal offence its enforcement will continue to cause harm. From a human rights perspective, more important than the practical understanding that these laws are largely ineffective in terms of deterrence, are the ever pervasive abuses of civil liberties in the name of prohibiting personal drug use. The argument for law

103

reform based on asserted rights and freedoms is expressed in the following statement by cannabis activist, Umberto Iorfida. Iorfida is emphatic in his characterization of marijuana prohibition as a violation of democratic principles that is worthy of fighting to change. He argues: "...It's on the same level as when blacks had to fight for equal rights, as when women had to fight for equal rights, as when disabled people had to fight for equal rights. It's the same category of human and civil rights that exists in any oppressed group, because that's what the marijuana smoker is.... We're not referred to as a member of the community, a pillar of salt, an industrious hardworking person. We're referred to as some unworthy scum, and that is oppression, and that oppression is because of the disinformation that has been taught throughout the years."

"To remove the disinformation would remove the prejudice. To remove the prejudice would mean that the rest of society can get on with life as well as those that are oppressed. And lifting the hammer of oppression I think is something that we have to continue to develop, because if we don't then we truly do not have equal rights for all. Equal rights for all means exactly that, equal rights for all, not some are more equal than others. Canada is the sum of all its people, not just some of its people. And the marijuana user has been excluded from virtually everything—excluded from travel, excluded from getting a good paying job, excluded from various activities in the community. That's incredibly stupid. To eliminate that section of society from and render them nonproductive and nonworthy in their own estimate, to make a person feel that they have no worth, is the worst form of prejudice that can be projected upon an individual. And that's what the marijuana law does to people who use marijuana. It reduces them to subhuman. It reduces them to subcitizenship."

"That is prejudice, that is hatred, and that is against the human rights bill not just of Canada, but the globe.... That, I think, is something worthy of fighting against and fighting to change.... That's no different than saying that a woman is not equal because she's a woman. That's no different than saying a black person is not equal because of their colour. To say that a person who uses marijuana is not equal because they use marijuana is just as bad. And that has to be removed from our conscious awareness, and it has to be removed from the books of legislation and law enforcement that allows that to occur. Because if it wasn't in the criminal books, it couldn't occur.... People who smoke marijuana are not worthless and that's the bottom line, and they need to be respected. We are as productive in society if allowed to be as anybody else and that is the tolerance level that we must achieve—the realization that even though a person smokes a joint of marijuana when they come home from work after a hard day, they can still get up the next morning and go back to work,

104

they can still earn money and provide tax base. They can still be useful in their community, they can still be useful in society, and they can still certainly contribute to the fabric of Canadian citizenship..."

Iorfida advocates "civil disobedience," fighting to change as opposed to simply breaking the law, as a means to "implement more modern concepts of solution" and bring about reform by way of the democratic process. Each citizen of Canada, he reminds us, has the same voting power as any other and can influence policy such that, once voting age has been reached, "...democracy allows each one of us to engage in change and modernization of our society." Iorfida is faithful that "in a democratic society we the people are also the government" and politicians are citizens just like anybody else; "...they have just been invoked with the power to act upon certain regulations and jurisdictions that are found to be acceptable by the majority." Accordingly, he argues, "...if the citizens relay to the politicians that we would like certain laws changed, then the politicians basically have no choice but to change those laws...government in itself becomes the inevitable mechanism that will affect the changes."

To affect the needed changes in tolerance to evolve social policies pertaining to cannabis, Iorfida is adamant as to the role of "educators" in our society to lead the way where politicians and other professionals, fearing the career implications of such a move—understandably so in most cases—have been afraid to take a stand. He said: "...if they can teach understanding as opposed to reefer madness fear, then you have a different type of interaction between the educators and those that are learning. And those that are learning are basically society. Starting off as children we teach a certain thing, then the children as they grow believe that certain thing, and they then project it onto their children and others in their community. If we teach tolerance, then that is what they will project. But if the educators are not comfortable with teaching the tolerance, then it will continue in the same course...more conducive to that tolerance, instead of the concept of don't do it just because we said that it's bad: 'Here is the actual and real medical research and scientific research; this is what it will do to you.' From there each individual person has a freedom of choice and a freedom of responsibility, and I believe that most adults are in fact responsible."

Such a liberal conception of tolerance, and the associated links between education and politics suggested by a number of informants in this study, assumes that change is possible from within the existing political system. Iorfida's arguments, for some, may seem misguided or even inappropriate, when given in comparison to more widely acknowledged targets and goals of the civil rights movement. In different terms perhaps than academics might express them, they are eloquently supportive of the following idea. Assuming the diffusion of accurate scientific knowledge to all members of the public through the education system (which brings to mind the stepping stone analogy suggested as a function of the harm reduction movement), legal rights for drug users could become an ethical focus in a way that more pragmatic reforms could not. New civil rights, notes Mitchell (1990) as in the development of legal rights for women, minorities, and more recently homosexuals, are normally rejected as odd, frightening, or laughable; so it is not altogether surprising that the idea of drug users having rights should be so politically volatile.

Taking human rights seriously involves a primary commitment to fairness and legal equality, implying a need for further elaboration and projection of the constitutional arguments available to reformers. These same arguments, with reference to the legal-political stalemate that hinders the advancement of cannabis policy in Canada, are addressed in more detail later in this chapter. But first it is important to develop liberalism as the predominant moral tradition from which a human rights view may be argued. The next section looks at central themes of liberal philosophers Immanuel Kant and J.S. Mill, who first articulated liberalism as a moral philosophy that upholds respect for personal autonomy and tolerance as ultimate "ends in themselves." At the risk of disappointing those readers who might rightfully demand a much more detailed explanation, I limit the analysis to just a few short pages that borrowing 'liberally' from more elegant and qualified discussions cited for their reference below.

**Invoking the Liberal Tradition**[*]

Although its roots may be traced to earlier traditions and cultures, most notably to aspects of Greek political thought and practice rejected by Aristotle, modern liberalism was born in the Enlightenment repudiation of all traditions in the name of humanistic reason (MacIntyre 1988). The humanist project of Kant and other early liberal philosophers centred on self-actualization in the rational pursuit of humanity as an end in itself. As noted by Wong (1984), the individualist turn to 'rights-centred' morality can be at least partly understood as the undermining of earlier moralities founded on notions of 'virtue' and a 'common good' that is discernable to all reasoning individuals. The latter aim is constituted by a system of roles specifying the contribution of each member to the shared life of the community. In this basic structure, virtues are the qualities necessary for

[*] This section is developed in additional detail in Hathaway, A.D. 2002. From Harm Reduction to Human Rights: Bringing Liberalism Back into Drug Reform Debates. Drug and Alcohol Review 21(4): 397-404.

the successful performance of roles in pursuit of the common good.

Through the practice of virtue, individuals provide the foundations of human community, seeking the common good within a cultural context defined by traditions of which their lives are a part. With modern science and the birth of individualism, however, came the rejection of Aristotelian conceptions of the good and attempts to justify virtues with their source in moral traditions. Most modern individuals can no longer see themselves as members of a community with a tradition and roles that determine their social identities. From the standpoint of modern individualism, one is what one chooses to be. Notions of a common good and shared life are not central to contemporary rights-centred morality. The emphasis instead is on rights belonging to each person, such as individual freedom and equality, and what each is entitled to claim from other members of the community (Wong 1984).

With the turn from virtue to rights-centred morality, a new social and cultural artifact was defined, that of 'the individual.' This defining development in liberal philosophy is summed up cogently by MacIntyre (1988, p. 339): "In Aristotelian practical reasoning it is the individual *qua* citizen who reasons...but in the practical reasoning of liberal modernity it is the individual *qua* individual who reasons." In modern liberal culture, the range of desired goods and individual preferences is irrevocably heterogeneous and without determinable order such that no overall theory of the human good can be regarded as justified. The practical rationality of liberalism as a modern moral and political philosophy is traditionally manifested in utilitarian terms fostering a neutral conception of the good and the idea of a rational calculus that can maximize satisfaction of individual preferences.

As noted with regards to harm reduction in chapter four (see Mugford 1993), however, utilitarianism cannot solve the problems of aggregating harm, nor has it ever solved the problem of aggregating different types of pleasure and happiness (MacIntyre 1981). To reiterate a previous contention, since excitement and pleasure are benefits not easily defended by way of harm reduction arguments, a utilitarian calculus, seeking to uphold "the greatest happiness for the greatest number," inevitably drifts towards the evaluation of costs alone. "In the case of illicit drugs, such a position necessarily drifts towards anti-drug, even prohibitionist sentiments" (Mugford 1993, p. 28). According to MacIntyre (1988, p. 343), debates at this level are necessarily barren; "...rival appeals to accounts of the human good or of justice necessarily assume a rhetorical form such that it is as assertion and counterassertion, rather than as argument and counterargument, that rival standpoints confront one another."

In the absence of tradition, he continues, there can be no rationality. At any fundamental level, there is no set of independent standards of rational justification by appeal to which the issues between opposing traditions can be decided, nor can a tradition be modified in any radical way. Where the preferences of different individuals and groups conflict in liberal culture and decisions are made as to which kinds of preference have priority over others, the need for some rational conception of justice by which to justify that order requires continuous debate on the principles of justice. The debates are perpetually inconclusive as to these basic principles, however, for it is here that the debates between liberals begin. A primary tenet of liberalism, Mill's widely debated "harm principle" put forward in his classic treatise On Liberty (1859), will be examined further with reference to a legal challenge of Canada's cannabis laws. In the case examined, the harm principle was ruled inadmissible as a principle of fundamental justice granting individuals the right to substance use .

More to the present point, liberalism is understood not as a rationality independent of tradition but as a tradition in itself with its own problematic set of questions. These problems, like all other moral and social traditions, it is committed to resolving by its own internal set of standards. Notwithstanding the liberal illusion of neutral standing, which suggests there can be a rationality independent of traditions, the person outside all tradition lacks the critical resources for rational inquiry. But to genuinely adopt the standpoint of a tradition prohibits one from adopting any rival standpoint. And so "...modern liberalism, born of antagonism to all tradition, has transformed itself gradually into what is now clearly recognizable even by some of its adherents as one more tradition" (MacIntyre 1988, p. 10).

From the fact that liberalism cannot provide a neutral ground independent of tradition from which to evaluate rival claims of practical rationality and justice, though it is the strongest claimant to provide such ground, MacIntyre concludes there is no rationality or justice as such, only the rationality and justice of this or that tradition. Whereas no rational debate between traditions can occur, conflicting ideas within a tradition may still share enough of the same fundamental beliefs to conduct such debates. Noting the contemporary debates within modern political systems are almost exclusively between rival variants of liberalism—as in the opposing camps of conservative liberalism, liberal liberalism, and radical liberalism—however, MacIntyre finds little place for putting liberalism itself in question.

Although liberal theorists cannot agree upon any precise formulation of rational justice, they are largely agreed on what justice should be designed to achieve. Chief among these widely shared principles is the understanding that any inequality in the treatment of individuals requires justification. States MacIntyre (1988, p. 344): "Justice is *prima facie* egalitarian. The goods about which it is egalitarian in this way are those which, it is presumed, everyone values: freedom to express and to implement preferences and a share in the means required to make that implementation effective." Appeals to justice under liberalism are referred to the formal rules and procedures of a legal system that functions to enforce and sustain the established social order wherein disputes over justice are resolved without recourse to any overall theory of the common good.

The overriding good of modern liberal culture, for MacIntyre (1988, p. 345), "...is no more and no less than the continued sustenance of the liberal and political order," an order that presupposes the fiction of some shared, even though unformulable, universal standard of rationality and justice. Whereas the foregoing account would seem to offer little hope for conceptual innovation and change, there is cause to be more optimistic about the prospects for advancing our social and political institutions in accordance with the defining principles of liberalism. A key point of contention between liberals and their critics is located in the aforementioned distinction between virtue and rights-centred moralities and in the opposing conceptions of liberty upheld by their adherents.

Critics of liberalism (moral conservatives and Marxists, for example), pointing to liberal subjectivity about values and the refusal to commit to any singular vision of the human good, decry what modern individualism has cost us in terms of social cohesion and morality. However, Richards (1979, p. 482) argues that it is a mistake to suppose, as Marxists do, that judgements about how human rights should be exercised, justifying critical blame but not extensive interference, reflect liberal subjectivity about personal values. Such judgements are not subjective, he continues: "Rather, they invoke intersubjective standards of criticism subject to testing and some validation about matters of prudence and morality.... That we are debarred from more extensive interference is not because the judgments are subjective but because, normatively, respect for personal independence requires that the person must be the final judge of the validity of our criticisms."

The quest for individual liberty as a conscious political ideal has purportedly undermined our mutual stake in "positive liberty," that sense of self-direction and mastery over the appetites or lower parts of the self that was exalted as the true meaning of political freedom among ancient civilizations—the Greeks, the Jewish, the Chinese—invoking the freedom to participate in ruling as well as in being ruled in common pursuit of the good. From this point of view, the liberty of modern individuals is a morally destitute kind of "negative liberty," one founded on the freedom to do as one wishes without interference from others (see Wong 1984). Where the assumption is made that the rational ends of all higher "true selves" coincide in the pursuit of the same common good—that is, the quest for positive liberty—suppression of negative liberty is allowed on the grounds that conflicting ends of the lower selves must be restrained in order for the true self to gain mastery. In the name of this freedom, all rational individuals should be willing to sacrifice their "negative" freedoms for the common good of society.

An opposing conception of negative liberty, often attributed to Mill and his followers that will be adhered to throughout this discussion, suggests a society can only be truly free that recognizes the inviolability of negative liberty. The next section, borrowing from work by Richards (1979) and Wong's (1984) understanding of "moral relativity," the continuing liberal tradition is developed as an invaluable "living tradition" (Bellah et al. 1985). As a living tradition, liberalism seeks not to provide ready made solutions to moral problems, but rather to evolve in a continuous process of conceptual innovation and challenge, assuming authority to be publicly pursued as a common project towards the more humane cultivation of our right to autonomy. My primary aim is to provide a defensible standpoint from which to develop a rights based perspective on 'the drug problem' with reference to cannabis. With particular attention to constitutional debates in the Canadian legal-political context, this standpoint is based on a view of morality founded on tolerance and respect for autonomy as indispensable ends in themselves.

**Autonomy and Tolerance as Moral Ends in Themselves:** The foregoing discussion of virtue describes it as an absolutist conception of morality which, notwithstanding nostalgic appeals to the 'common good' and fading values of an earlier era, is difficult to defend in the present context of modern individualism. In spite of the critiques that stem from misinterpretation of moral relativism as nothing but the empty admonition to be free, liberalism (which denies there can be any singular conception of the good) is the most sustainable view of the essence of contemporary western morality. In the present context of liberalism, the failure of absolutist theories to explain the wide diversity and kinds of disagreement entailed in moral belief is most likely incurable (Wong 1984).

Morality is a social creation that is constantly evolving in response to the needs of human beings to resolve interpersonal conflicts of interest. Although there are certain constraints—consequent to our human nature, social environment, and standards of rationality in particular—on what a morality can be like and still serve our purposes, these constraints are not enough to eliminate all but one morality. Indeed, it is not

110

obvious that we need any moral absolutes by which to say who is absolutely right and wrong in every moral disagreement; nor is it obvious that we cannot learn to accept our moral beliefs as determined in part by our own specific history and social environment (Wong 1984).

A particular feature of modern Western culture is our growing awareness of a variety of lifestyles that may conflict with our own. More than ever before in our history, it is necessary to interact with those who have been shaped by different ways of life and to question our moral stance with regard to these others. Viewing morality as something that evolves in response to changing needs and the growing awareness of those needs, moral relativity is an indication of the elasticity of human nature and the adaptive power of our ways of living to determine what constitutes a satisfactory resolution of the conflicts morality is intended to resolve. At the same time, notes Wong (1984, p. 176): "Many of us seem to be caught between an attitude of greater toleration for other ways of life and an uneasy feeling that our own values are being eroded the more tolerant we become."

In response to this dilemma, for those who are committed to the idea of liberal tolerance, it does not follow that moral relativity has no further implications in terms of how we deal with those who practice a different morality that may be as valid as our own. Accordingly, Wong (1984, p. 178) maintains that: "Tolerance must be defended from the standpoint of some moral system, not from a morally neutral one." Far from the abdication or partial endorsement of all established moralities, tolerance is a value of a particular kind of morality, a moral value unto itself. To transcend the current focus, leaving the finer points to be argued between philosophers, a demonstration of how moral relativism is possible as a viable and coherent moral standpoint is distilled from Wong's answer to the following conundrum: In the name of tolerance, must we tolerate intolerance? Arguing from a standpoint of absolute moral relativism, one forsaking all moral systems must begrudgingly affirm this conclusion.

For those who have come to believe in moral relativism in the context of a culture that emphasizes individual autonomy, however, there are clear moral warrants to reject the conclusion. Not only is it consistent with the relativist argument in this context to condemn the intolerance of others, even though their intolerance may be justifiable to them, we may also take steps to prevent their intolerance. A noteworthy distinction between unobtrusive condemnation versus outright prevention of intolerance, and important political strength of liberalism, is found in the liberal defense of the free speech rights of intolerant groups to communicate their intolerance. Richards (1979, p. 472) argues: "That even such groups, who may deny in

111

principle the liberal imperative of treating persons as equals, should have the right to communicate is a forceful and striking reminder of the vigorous conception of civic courage and personal independence which liberalism enshrines, including the ongoing willingness...to extend, even to the intolerant, a concern and respect which they deny to others."

Even if a communication is offensive or clearly false to others, the liberal response is not prohibition, but open rebuttal by which persons are compelled to self-critically understand and evaluate the rational grounds of their beliefs. As stated by Wong (1984, pp. 189-190): "The argument does seem to imply a *prima facie* duty not to interfere with them, but if we are committed to promoting tolerance, then we must ask whether our interference is a lesser evil than letting them impose their will on others. We would have to weigh conflicting *prima facie* duties, both derived from the value of tolerance. It would not be a contradiction to conclude that our commitment to that value weighed in favor of interference." The theme of individual autonomy is a central and pervasive one in the moral traditions of Europe and in cultures descending from Europe. Thus, returning to Kant's liberal philosophy of humanity as an end in itself, we have compelling and viable grounds to uphold a moral conception of tolerance.

A clear implication of Kant's (1785) formula is that we should refrain from interfering with the permissible ends of others. That the ends are permissible is a necessary qualification in the sense that others may have immoral ends that justify interference. In the Enlightenment spirit of reason, Kant's permissible ends are rational ends, implying one should not interfere with the ends of others unless one can justify the interference to them as rational beings fully informed of all relevant circumstances. Since the core of Kant's theory (reinterpreted in Mill's (1859) articulation of the 'harm principle') is that persons as individuals have a natural capacity for self-critical rationality about their lives and how they are lived, Wong's (1984) argument for moral relativity on the grounds of personal autonomy is compelling. Richards (1979) observes that whereas Kant goes further than Mill towards explicating the moral requirement of treating persons as equals in terms of this human capacity, the two are clearly united in their emphasis on autonomy.

The case for developing a human rights argument in support of the right to use cannabis is thus a corollary of the Kantian liberal tradition of treating persons as equals by virtue of their autonomy. By Richards' (1979, p. 468) definition: "The idea of human rights, without begging the question of what is the good for any particular person, secures the minimum condition which enable persons, with the dignity of freedom and rationality, to design their lives...to face the highest creative task of human life—to make a life.

To this extent, rights...are defined independently of the good, and define the boundary of constraints within which people on fair terms are free to define their own good." Unlike earlier moral traditions emphasizing a good that is common to all individuals, liberalism frees the individual to pursue her or his own way of living through the cultivation of capacities of self-critical independence. The task of the person is not blankly unguided, but rather confronted with a lively and critical culture of contending traditions.

Making choices between different rival traditions calls for the deepening development of self-critical capacities of rational autonomy, marked by liberalism's concern for the basic education of all persons. Such concerns centre not only on basic schooling, but on the general availability of access to critical traditions which enable people to deepen their capacities to self-critically assess and change their lives in an experimentally creative and humane way. The liberal concern with education, and how to best live one's life through the humane cultivation of rights, does not arise in a vacuum. States Richards (1979, p. 485): "The liberal theory of rights depends on a background theory of justice, which establishes as one fundamental right the right to education and culture, which is intended to facilitate the kind of independence which can invoke and exercise rights...both education and politics are guided by the same focal values." The most fundamental right of liberalism is that persons are to be treated as equals by virtue of their individual autonomy. Accordingly, its central concern lies in clarifying the link between the autonomy based interpretation of treating persons as equals and the content of specific rights that are guaranteed to persons under constitutional democracy.

An important task of liberalism is to make treating people as equals the central tenet of constitutional morality. Following Mill's (1859) argument, liberal principles warrant interference with personal autonomy only when the agent's actions harm the interests of others. As noted by Richards (1979), whereas Mill clearly believed in a just scope for paternalism—in the case of children, and even adults in cases of extreme irrationality posing serious harm to human interests—his objection to the tyranny of majoritarian convention, and abuse of paternalistic arguments to justify state interference, led him to formulate the harm principle with dramatic simplicity. Beyond the scope of principles treating persons as equals, Mill saw a general right of autonomy, meaning the only end for which the coercive power of the state can be rightfully exercised over the individual is restricted to the prevention of harm. In particular, there is no justifiable ground for interfering with personal autonomy in the interests of the agent only. Given the importance of individual autonomy, we ought never to interfere except for the sake of preventing harm to others; any more interference is not only

113

ineffective but counterproductive. Individuals are morally free to decide whether and how to exercise their rights of autonomy.

Again, this is not to say that criticism is unjustified—only coercive interference. People may still take critical attitudes toward the exercise of rights, some of them grounded in prudence and others in moral ideals. According to Richards (1979, p. 480): "Criticism of others, based on such an ideal, serves exactly the purposes moral ideals should serve, making people self-critically consider how more humanely to exercise their rights. On the other hand, enforcement of such an ideal, via the morality of the criminal law, would clearly violate human rights...assuming as a necessary personal value what may, for an individual, be oppressive and exploitative." Thus the availability of criticism is a natural way in which the exercise of one's rights may be more self-critically informed. Whereas such an approach recognizes the exercise of rights as being not infallible, yet malleable through the self-critical assessment of outside moral criticism, criticism of others should be limited due to the likelihood of mistaken judgements concerning the life circumstances and ends of another.

Critical judgements of another, argues Richards (1979), often are failures of imagination to understand his or her special relation to life and to sensitively assess the indeterminacy of values. Such distortions are particularly apparent where a prior history of unjustified moralism tends to disfigure realistic perceptions of the exercise of rights to personal autonomy. With respect to arguing for the right to use drugs, with Richards (1979, p. 485), I contend that: "Liberalism's focal concern with self-critical dignity in choosing a life is not concerned to deny the constraints which such choices must take into account, but to insure that only those constraints are accepted which are reasonable to the person and which relate to the individuality of one's person and context." Naturally, this begs the question of what is meant by notions like 'reasonable constraint' within a given context. A narrower focus is accordingly pursued here to examine marijuana prohibition in the specific Canadian context of law and society. In exploring the constitutional arguments available under the *Charter of Rights and Freedoms*, I revisit the harm principle in light of a court ruling that struck down a legal challenge put forward on that basis to illuminate the grounds for subsequent appeals.

**Arguing Human Rights Under Constitutional Democracy**[*]

A human rights based commitment to legal equality and fairness calls upon traditional legal protections that put the onus on regulators to justify state intervention. Borrowing again from Mill's (1859) <u>On Liberty</u>, a basic tenet of liberalism holds that only public defense justifies state intervention or coercion. Accordingly, intervention should be limited to actions that threaten civil order or jeopardize public security; and repressive action should be limited to minimize disruption of citizen's rights. Some find in <u>On Liberty</u> a rights based concern for personal autonomy; however, the Anglo-American tradition opposing the overcriminalization of drug use has typically relied on efficiency-based utilitarian arguments. These latter forms deplore and target the counterproductive use of scarce resources in enforcing laws that govern moral conduct. The utilitarian critique of overcriminalization, stemming from Mill's (1859, 1863) original theses, follows a well-known liberal doctrine that has come to be known as the harm principle.

In compliance with the harm principle, the scope of criminal law is limited such that acts may be made criminal only if they inflict concrete harm on assignable persons. Moreover, it is never proper to criminalize an act solely on the grounds of preventing harm to the agent or because the mere thought of the act is offensive to others. Although Mill valued the idea of 'rational autonomy' as a means to encourage innovations enabling people to realize more pleasure in their lives, however, his utilitarian calculus lacks the moral foundation that is needed to give personal autonomy decisive weight over concerns for solidarity and security. As noted by Richards (1982), decriminalization arguments typically concede the immorality of such conduct and then go on to discuss the excessive costs of preventing it. In practice, however, efficiency based arguments have had little success in reducing the scope of decriminalized conduct.

Where decriminalization has occurred (in the case of contraception, abortion, and consensual sexual relations between adults, for example), it has resulted from a shift in moral judgements rather than cost efficiency assessments *per se* (Richards 1982). Where existing moral judgements have remained unchallenged, movement toward decriminalization has been negligible. Lacking adequate expression of personal autonomy as a moral value in itself, the utilitarian conception of the harm principle is vulnerable to attack from arguments justifying state paternalism and the enforcement of morals (e.g., Hart 1963, Devlin

---

[*] This section is developed in additional detail in Hathaway, A.D. 2001. Charter Rights of Canadian Drug Users: A Constitutional Assessment of the Clay Trial and Ruling. <u>Canadian Journal of Law and Society</u> 16(1): 29-43.

115

1965). Situating this contention in the context of ongoing end of the last century drug policy debates, we will consider a 1990's court challenge and decision concerning the right to use cannabis. But first we go back further to earlier deliberations, to provide a fuller understanding of positions on the proper role of government in controlling personal drug use.

The report of the LeDain Commission of Inquiry into the Non-Medical Use of Drugs (1972), reaching majority consensus on a wide range of observations and findings on cannabis, recommended the drug be decriminalized for simple possession and use. The majority report presented an assortment of recommendations combining treatment and punishment options that would retain the criminal status of drugs other than cannabis while supporting provisions for assistance and treatment of users rather than punishment for simple possession. Because of its low toxicity, the LeDain majority position demanded that cannabis be decriminalized but not legalized, so as still to deter young people from the habits and harms they are apt to inflict on themselves. Based on a position presented previously by Hart (1963), it is argued that the criminal law has a paternalistic function. This justifies restricting rights in order to preserve social order and protect persons from harms they may do to themselves. Thus the state has the right to restrict access to drugs, through forceful means if necessary, to prevent individuals from doing harm to themselves and society.

The above contentions favouring paternalism on the part of the majority of LeDain commissioners is balanced by two minority positions—one of them more liberal and the other more conservative concerning need for civil rights and social control measures. The more conservative conception of drug control policy put forward by Ian Campbell argued that not only does the state have a paternalistic function as guardian of public order; it is also a safeguard of social morality. Advancing a similar view to Lord Devlin's (1965)—who is best known for opposing a movement in Britain to change the laws against homosexuality and prostitution—Campbell insists that the state is responsible for enforcing conventional morality on drug use regardless of actual harm. In the case of cannabis, he demands criminal penalties be upheld as with any behaviour that is seen as a threat to established morality.

In defense of prohibiting simple possession of cannabis, Campbell states further: "It seems to me an unassailable proposition that the majority may properly prohibit through the law conduct that is manifestly offensive or disturbing to them whether or not that conduct inflicts an injury on any particular person beyond the actor.... There is every reason to think that the public use of cannabis is offensive and disturbing to the vast majority of Canadians. There is even more reason to think that public use by young people is particularly

116

offensive. Hence, it appears not inappropriate that such behavior should be forbidden by law.... It seems to me that recently we have been far too little concerned with the consequences of placing too many rights and freedoms on the shoulders of the young" (LeDain 1972, pp. 312-314). Because the marijuana laws in Canada have not changed much since the LeDain majority report, they more embody Campbell's view supporting the enforcement of morality through influence of law.

Forty years after LeDain one might argue that state intervention, justified in the name of paternalism and protecting values, has moved toward further repression and violation of the civil rights of substance users. The only position that would enable such repression to be avoided, Beauchesne (1991) argues, is one founded on respect for civil liberties. Such a sharply contrasting view of drug policy, following Mill's liberal conception of the state as guardian of public order only, was presented in the LeDain minority report of Commissioner Marie Bertrand. She called for limiting state intervention to the sale of adulterated drugs and other such demonstrable threats to public security, while suggesting any intervention at all in the case of private drug use is intolerable, a clear violation of citizens' rights. From a human rights view of drug use, the laws against cannabis are clearly abusive of the powers bestowed on the state by the people. Accordingly, not only are the drug laws unjustified as a means of enforcing morality, they cannot be justified on paternalistic grounds either.

For the law to have a pedagogical function, notes Beauchesne (1991) citing Bertrand, it must be consistent and proportional to the harm it seeks to prevent. Moreover, she wonders, in what way such a function is demonstrated for the many thousands of young people arrested in Canada each year for simple possession of cannabis. Mitchell (1990) agrees that while freedom of drug choice should not depend upon proof of harmlessness, the drug laws are unethical because they unfairly distinguish between drugs and unfairly distinguish between drug use and other socially harmful behaviours. If psychoactive drug use were subject to a broadly uniform system of regulation based on equality, proportionality of harm, democratic choice and fairness, argues Mitchell (1988), turning to a cost-benefit analysis within the constraints of justice, we would find general agreement between the two analytical frameworks.

He adds, if we are to accept the empirical evidence as to the actual harms posed by illicit as opposed to presently accepted drug solutions, fairness demands that all psychoactives be treated equally. Whereas equality itself does not determine what system of control should be applied, nor that all drug users should be treated identically, all would be subject to the same general controls. Thus it would be just as 'fair' if the

117

criminal law were to prohibit all such drug use on penalty of death as it would if no drugs were prohibited. Whatever the exact outcome of attempts to reschedule drugs and controls uniformly based on proportionality and fairness, Mitchell suggests it would force individuals and legislators to include their own drug use and abuse in their political calculations. Hence relying too heavily on cost-benefit arguments may well be a strategic mistake of reformers.

Combining both radical and traditional messages, human rights based arguments are self-consciously political and make far more sense given that courts, judges, jurors, and legislators are accustomed to thinking in terms of rights (Mitchell 1990). Again, Mitchell reminds us that new rights, as in civil rights for women, homosexuals, and racial minorities, for example, are normally rejected as peculiar or frightening to begin with. Unlike racial or sexual characteristics, however, drug use is discretionary. A better fitting comparison to drug use may be found in our individual freedom of choice of religion and politics. In a heterogeneous society, he states, the necessary preventative to civil war is religious and political freedom. Demands for law reform centring on harm reduction and other efficiency-based arguments against moralistic paternalism are thereby ancillary to establishing a rights-based morality that upholds the freedom to use drugs as a right worthy of protection by our courts and legislatures.

**Rights and Freedoms of Drug Users Under the Charter:** As noted by Mitchell (1988), whereas the *Charter of Rights and Freedoms*—Part I of the 1982 *Constitution Act* hereafter referred to as the *Charter*—states that everyone has such "fundamental freedoms" as "freedom of conscience and religion" and "freedom of thought, belief, opinion and expression," no formula is provided by which the selection of particular rights and exclusion of others is explainable. In this context, he continues, the right to use one's drug of choice can be promoted in one of two ways: "First, such a right or freedom can simply be proclaimed as part of the basic rights package. If such a proclamation is lacking, the second possibility is to argue that a specified right, such as the 'right to liberty' guaranteed in section 7 of the *Charter*, extends far enough to cover the disputed action" (Mitchell 1988, p. 424). In the U.S., argues Mitchell, due to strong court biases in drug matters and a general reluctance to overrule duly elected legislators, attempts to rule out drug prohibition on constitutional grounds have failed despite the empirical accuracy and logic of the arguments presented.

Similarly in Canada, it is perhaps unrealistic to expect the *Charter* to resolve the many conflicts and inconsistencies in drug legislation. The precarious balance between the need for enforcement and the individual rights of drug users will no doubt continue for some time to come (Erickson and Blackwell 1988).

118

After almost thirty years since the *Charter* was enacted, those who expected a sudden transformation in drug law enforcement are surely disappointed. Indeed, note Erickson and Blackwell (1988), it has taken some time since the passage of the *Charter* and will take some time yet for interpretations and decisions from case law to accumulate, none of which can be deemed conclusive unless favourably arbitrated and delivered by the Supreme Court of Canada. Nonetheless, it gives the courts the means to rigorously protect a widening array of individual rights and freedoms. In particular, argues Solomon (1988), certain search powers and tactics used in drug enforcement will be struck down or limited by the *Charter* which provides, for the first time, a public forum wherein drug enforcement policies and practices can be openly discussed. After ten more years of accumulated case law, the former point made by Solomon is reiterated in the following excerpt from our 1998 interview.

While there are self-serving aspects to our legal system acting to limit the scope of *Charter* protections, it has been largely effective as a means to combat some of the more "outrageous features" of drug law enforcement. Professor Solomon explains: "What the *Charter* has done is it has taken the hard edge off some of the more outrageous features of drug enforcement, but it has taken the edge off selectively. If you look at where the courts have been aggressive in terms of the *Charter*...our courts are not particularly concerned about throatholds where RCMP officers grab people who they think might be carrying drugs.... They have authorized, at least initially, rectal examinations; no orifice is too private in which to search for the demon drugs. They have no difficulty with unannounced entry. Where the courts tend to get exercised is in warrantless search. Why? Because judges issue warrants, right to counsel. Why? Because the court thinks that lawyers are at the forefront and judges are at the forefront.... So there's that kind of self-serving stuff, but I tend to think that the *Charter* has taken the hard edge off some of the most outrageous features of drug enforcement."

In the excerpt below, drawing comparisons between drug use and constitutional protections such as freedom of religion and expression, autonomy and security of the person (as in the right to abortion), and the "right to liberty" guaranteed under section 7 of the *Charter*, Solomon argues any rational analysis of relative harm cannot justify criminalizing simple possession of a drug such as cannabis. Assuming the debate around drugs were rational, to be consistent with other currently protected *Charter* rights and freedoms, the courts would have to recognize drug use within the same realm of private decision making. But that would assume the debate around drugs is rational. In Solomon's words: "...I think we can move a long way. I mean, I think at

119

a certain point you have to decide where it is that you want to get to. It's very interesting in our society the kind of blatant hypocrisies that exist: You are a Jehovah's Witness. You believe that if you get blood, you will be damned to an eternity in Hell, and we will let you die for your religious beliefs and religious convictions. We will not treat you against your will."

"Now, is there any objective proof that you're going to be damned to an eternity in Hell if you take blood? No. So, the autonomy of the individual will protect you where you make a decision which we know with certainty will result in your death, but God help you if you smoke a joint. Did I miss something in this equation? ...The right to security of the person allows you to have an abortion and kill a viable fetus. It allows you to...adopt a lifestyle that we know will inflict on the child you've decided to carry to term horrible handicaps. But if you smoke a joint, we'll kick open the door and send you to prison. I don't get it. If the right to liberty in section 7 protects personal decision making, and it seems to me if the state wants to intervene, it should do so in a principled fashion. If the state were to say, 'No, no, no—the state won't intervene unless your decision is too stupid for words;' so if they wanted to draw the barrier in terms of life, and life and death decisions, and did it consistently, I could understand that. But it doesn't. It makes no sense..."

"I am overwhelmingly of the view that if section 7 allows you to die for your religious beliefs, if you can have an abortion—if a law prohibiting access to abortion interferes with your right to life, liberty, and security as a person—if the courts recognize a realm of private decision making in the area of health and autonomy, then there is no way you can justify our current laws criminalizing possession of many drugs which are now illicit...any honest analysis of the relative harms of consumption of marijuana to some of the things that you're allowed to do.... Shit, you're allowed to bungee jump, we have professional boxing in our society, we have high speed automobile racing, we have the World Wrestling Federation (I mean that should be banned on bad taste alone). But that would assume the debate is rational, and the debate around drugs has never been rational."

"Judges and Supreme Courts don't smoke marijuana, at least not that I'm aware of. Now, my guess is they drink scotch, and my guess is some of them smoke and their friends smoke. A drug problem can be defined very clearly in terms of the drugs that other people use; that's how you define a drug problem. Because if I use it, it ain't a problem." Despite the biases of alluded to by Solomon, and regardless of the outcome the challenge, a *Charter* challenge focuses attention in open court on whether constitutional rights and freedoms have been violated. Solomon (1988) notes changes made by police and prosecutors in their practices to avoid constitutional challenges may actually do more to effect the safeguarding of rights than the successful court challenges themselves. Moreover, the *Charter* encourages us to fundamentally reexamine Canadian drug control policy, and may indeed induce Parliament to more carefully consider the question of individual rights when drafting statutes.

Since the final report of the LeDain Commission nearly four decades ago, a legal-political stalemate has arisen leaving the cannabis reform movement in limbo, awaiting other opportunities to press the issue back into the judicial or political forum. Steadfast resistance on the part of law defenders has proven all the more resilient in view of the apparent 'easy out' option open to courts and legislatures of passing challenges back and forth between the two forums. The present impasse is described by law professor Alan Young in this excerpt from our interview in 1998: "...I have absolutely no confidence in the political forum. I think that this issue has been primarily characterized by legislative inertia. They've had so many opportunities to address it and haven't. So I use my skills as a lawyer to shift it out of the political forum into the judicial forum, all with the expectation that with the proper press coverage we would be able to push it back into the legislative forum, because I never really expected to get favourable responses from courts."

Although constitutional challenges are expensive to launch and would seem to stand little chance of success legally, Young underscores their importance in maintaining the media spotlight and public attention on the cannabis issue, "...because the press is very interested in the issue, and if the press is interested and the public is interested, the politicians may have to respond." Citing recent international developments in progressive law reform and a general interest in society regarding recreational drug use, Young characterizes the revival of the cannabis movement as a "Renaissance period" in which, following the more repressive drug policy "dark ages" of the Reagan and Bush eras, public discussion and debate on the issue has been able to once more ensue. Since interest in drug consumption and policy ebbs and flows over time, Young suggests the timing of challenges is crucial, and that the socio-political climate of the late 1990's was an opportunity for law reformers to take advantage of favourable public opinion and press coverage. One such effort backed by Young, a constitutional challenge of Canadian cannabis law hereinafter referred to as R. v Clay, is outlined below with the aim to analyze key discursive elements of the landmark trial and ruling.

**The Clay Trial and Ruling:** In May of 1995, former hemp shop proprietor Chris Clay was arrested and charged with cultivation and possession for the purpose of trafficking after selling small cannabis plant cuttings in his London, Ontario store. Although he had operated *Hemp Nation*, Canada's first hemp store,

121

openly selling marijuana seeds, waterpipes, and other paraphernalia for two years previously, local police finally decided he had 'pushed the envelope' too far and laid a number of charges. After enlisting the counsel of Professor Alan Young, who in 1994 fought successfully to strike down part of the criminal code prohibiting promotion or sale of illicit drug literature (Iorfida v MacIntyre, 21 O.R. (3d) pp. 186-205), Clay launched his own constitutional challenge of Canada's cannabis laws. Raising funds primarily through donations collected via his *Hemp Nation* website, Clay was able to raise the money required to bring in expert witnesses from across North America.

For three weeks during the spring of 1997, the court heard testimony from over a dozen prominent witnesses (including several key informants who took part in this study) representing a diverse range of fields, including pharmacology, sociology, criminology, psychiatry, and law among others. In the interest of brevity, the key arguments and verdict taken from the final ruling of Judge John McCart (delivered orally August 14, 1997) is herein presented with an eye to delineate certain discrepancies between his factual and constitutional assessments of the case. McCart's ruling, I will argue, is indicative of the limits to factual argumentation and the need for further development and articulation of constitutional arguments available under the *Charter*.

The challenge launched by Clay before the Provincial Court of Ontario sought a stay of proceedings on the judgement of charges faced by the applicant on the basis that they violated section 7 of the *Charter*. Section 7 provides that: "Everyone has the right to life, liberty and security of the person, and the right not to be deprived thereof except in accordance with the principles of fundamental justice." Thus the matter to be deliberated, as stated by McCart at the outset of his verdict: "...has there been a deprivation of one or more of these rights, and if so, was the deprivation contrary to the principles of fundamental justice?" The burden of proof was thereby placed on the applicants to demonstrate each of several constitutional issues raised by the challenge—chief among which, for present purposes at least, whether it is a violation of the principles of fundamental justice for Parliament to prohibit, upon threat of criminal sanction, conduct which is relatively harmless, and to thereby interfere with an individual's right to make autonomous decisions in the absence of compelling reasons for the interference.

In his factual assessment of the arguments presented, largely agreeing with the evidence as to the "relative harmlessness" of cannabis, Justice McCart concluded "...as it is commonly used, occasionally, cannabis presents only minor or subtle risks to the health of the individual." While consumption of marijuana is not completely harmless, citing in particular the risk of pulmonary damage consequent to heavy use,

122

McCart accepted as valid the general consensus among experts that moderate use of the drug causes no physical or psychological harm and is unlikely to create serious harm for most users or society. On summary review of the cannabis law reforms that have taken place in western Europe and Australia, he stated further: "The national governments of Canada and the United States appear to be somewhat out of step with most of the Western world." In addition, citing a 1995 Health Canada report that found 27 percent of Canadians believe marijuana possession should be legal, and 42.1 percent believe it should be punishable by fine or non-jail sentence only, McCart observed that 70 percent of Canadians would seem to support a change in the existing law.

On the other hand, he argued, a significant majority of Canadians do not believe marijuana possession should be legal. Moreover, although penalties have been eased in several other countries, in most cases possession of marijuana was still against the law and nowhere in the western world had cultivation, trafficking or possession for the purpose of trafficking been decriminalized. All of the so-called decriminalization initiatives in the Netherlands and elsewhere, notes McCart, were legislative initiatives, not court imposed; therefore the changes requested by the applicants regarding simple possession and small-scale cultivation of cannabis constituted "...an unwarranted intrusion into the legislative domain." Despite reaching a conclusion based on his assessment of the factual evidence that would seem to support the call for decriminalization, the constitutional challenge was dismissed on the grounds that there is no "principle of fundamental justice" to warrant the intrusion.

Although invested with the power to rule on whether the laws pertaining to marijuana are constitutional or not, McCart maintained the easing of restrictions on simple possession and use of the drug rests firmly within the legislative domain. Section 52 of the *Charter* states any law that is inconsistent with the provisions of the Constitution is "...to the extent of the inconsistency, of no force and effect." Judges are thereby invested with the power to measure any law against broadly worded rights and freedoms guaranteed by the *Charter*. While there are those who welcome the new powers bestowed on superior courts as an essential safeguard of democracy in Canada, others decry the growth of "judicial activism" by unelected judges as threatening to parliament and due legislative process (see Bindman 1998). As made clear in his ruling on the case of R. v Clay, Judge McCart is unequivocally of the latter point of view. Judicial deference is appropriate, he argues, to guard against court interference where legislators have had to make difficult policy choices among conflicting alternatives. As for the principles of fundamental justice, these "...cannot be

123

created for the occasion to reflect the court's dislike or distaste of a particular statute."

Quoting extensively from a ruling by Justice John McClung (1996, Vriend v Alberta, 132 D.L.R. (4th) pp. 606-607), who warned against "ideologically driven...constitutionally hyperactive judges" usurping the proper function of democratically elected representatives of the people, McCart argued that the principles of fundamental justice leave a great deal of scope for personal judgement. In attempting to establish the meaning of the term, these principles were deemed 'fundamental' in the sense that they have general acceptance among reasonable people as being vital to our societal notion of justice. Whereas discerning the principles of fundamental justice with which deprivation of life, liberty, or security of the person must accord in order to withstand constitutional scrutiny is no easy task, notes McCart, fundamental justice requires a fair balance be struck between the interests of the person who claims his liberty has been violated and the protection of society at large.

Turning to address each of several constitutional issues raised by the applicants as to the designation of cannabis as a prohibited substance, with regard to the harm principle and right to personal autonomy, McCart ruled there does not exist a principle of fundamental justice to warrant any such intrusion into legislative matters. Finding no prior authority for the proposition that illegal conduct need cause actual harm before legislated against by Parliament—somewhat inconsistent with his earlier assessment of the factual claims of the applicants—McCart declared "...in any event...consumption of marijuana does cause harm, albeit and perhaps not as much harm as was first believed." Citing similar decisions in the United States and Canada, he argued that continuing questions about the drug and its effects make the classification rational, and therefore legislative action must be upheld as long as a rational basis for the classification still exists.

With respect to personal autonomy—that is, the applicants' claim that it is a violation of the principles of fundamental justice for Parliament to interfere with an individual's right to make autonomous decisions in the absence of compelling reasons to so intervene—McCart contends that freedom of the individual must be subjected to numerous constraints for the common good. And although it was agreed that liberty grants the individual a degree of autonomy in making decisions of fundamental personal importance, since "...marijuana is primarily used for occasional recreation. One might legitimately ask whether this form of recreation qualifies as of 'fundamental personal importance' such as to attract *Charter* attention." Backed by other major North American court decisions, McCart contended: "Few would believe they have been deprived of something of critical importance if deprived of marijuana." The *Charter*, he continues, does not protect

124

against such an insignificant or "trivial" limitation of rights.

Thus, to summarize McCart's assessment of the factual and constitutional claims presented, his initial position, following the general consensus as to the relative harmlessness of marijuana, is overturned by the ruling that it is nevertheless sufficiently harmful to justify government intervention. And that even if it were harmless, as a matter of public policy, it is still up to Parliament, not the courts, to decide. Furthermore, with reference to the "common good" that is generally accepted "among reasonable people," McCart remarked that such an insignificant limitation of rights is surely too trivial to be deserving of legislative scrutiny. In his closing arguments, he noted new provisions for "alternative measures" other than judicial proceedings in the Controlled Drugs and Substances Act suggest that "...Parliament is moving away from the harshness of the penalties for possession of marijuana...." Perhaps someday, he added, Canada might adopt some of the decriminalization measures that are practiced in Australia and western European nations, "...which I do not believe would meet with much objection from an informed public."

This constitutional assessment sheds new light on the observed state of legislative inertia that forestalls further advancement of the cannabis law reform issue in Canada. On review of the arguments herein presented in this and the chapters preceding, McCart's ruling supports the contention that rational arguments are less important than establishing a rights-based morality that upholds the freedom of drug use as being worthy of protection by courts and legislatures. Before concluding our analysis, a final word from Alan Young, who plainly states the matter—much as Mill did long before—of the need to put the onus on law makers to justify government intervention in the lives of its citizens. Inquiring about Young's strategy to appeal McCart's decision, how did he intend, I asked, to establish marijuana use as a fundamental right of enough importance to warrant constitutional protection? He replied: "I don't think I have to establish that it's of fundamental importance to warrant *Charter* attention. I've never understood that response which was the Crown's argument, and obviously the Judge accepted it as an easy way out of the difficult constitutional issue."

"I'd like to see what would happen if tomorrow the federal government outlawed golf and see if people would just say, 'Oh, it's not fundamentally important—it's only a recreational activity, who cares.' It's about liberty, absolutely principally about liberty; not about whether it's important. I mean it's not important to have potato chips.... The issue is whether or not Canadians should be treated as autonomous, free-willed individuals who are capable of making responsible choices. When certain products are so injurious to the

125

individual or to society at large that it's not worth giving people autonomous choice, then I can understand and be sympathetic to government intervention. But when a product has virtually no harm to the individual, and absolutely no harm to society as I see it, then I don't think we have to assess government intervention on the basis of whether it's important to Canadians. It's just a question of whether or not the government should have a constitutional right to interfere in autonomous choices that Canadians should be able to make...."

"Again, I'm not that confident in the ability of our Court of Appeal to respond favourably to my claim, so the overall strategy is to keep the issue alive.... And if the Court of Appeal endorses some of McCart's factual findings, again the public will be exposed to the hypocrisy of the law that we have this very punitive response to what seems to be very trivial, harmless activity.... So I will string it out as long as I can. I will rely upon as much rhetoric as I can to get newsworthy quotes. And it's all just about keeping the issue alive and trying to get a judgement that is as favourable as McCart's judgement. He was very weak on the law and he took the easy route out, but...he said he learned things in the trial he never thought he would hear. And he said that all the developments in the other countries have been motivated by proper information, and why we don't have change is because the proper information isn't out there yet."

"That was a remarkable thing to get out of a 75 year old...elderly, conservative judge. But...when he turned to the constitutional claims, he was effectively saying...there is no principle of constitutional law that Parliament can only act if they have a sound basis for believing that an activity is harmful...stated abstractly it sounds like he might be right. But when you start to give concrete examples...what's going to prevent Parliament tomorrow from creating a law prohibiting and criminalizing the cultivation of roses? There could be people having criminal records for cultivating roses, and are we saying that courts are powerless to intervene? Then what's the use of the *Charter*, quite frankly?"

**Summary**

The foregoing analysis of the Clay trial and ruling supports the idea that claims based on strictly rational arguments for cannabis law reform are rhetorically limiting insofar as they lack an established "beachhead of accepted principles" (Best 1987) from which to manoeuvre in legal-political forums. Whereas the harm reduction movement (with its claims-making style which was well-represented among the experts who testified), has short term advantages as a stepping stone toward long sought after policy reform, the matter of entitlement is central yet neglected. Harm reduction priorities, in Canada and elsewhere, are difficult to

126

reconcile with the self-consciously political warrants for change presented here. Although social norms of tolerance and respect for human rights are fundamental issues for the harm reduction movement, the need for marijuana law reform is easily trivialized in its rational scope of inquiry and practice.

As a matter of strategy, I have accordingly expounded a morally grounded approach to the argument wherein the rights of the person to pursue his or her own ends without undue interference take on primary significance. Borrowing from the classic works of Kant and Mill, and other contributions in the liberal tradition, I have defended liberalism as *the* moral tradition, upholding the right to use drugs on the basis of respect for personal autonomy and tolerance as moral ends in themselves. In Canada, and other western nations, it was noted that efforts to determine the meaning of vague "principles of fundamental justice" are precisely where the debates within liberalism begin. Arguing human rights under constitutional democracy in Canada appeals to fundamental rights and freedoms (especially the right to "liberty and security of the person") that are guaranteed by the *Charter*.

As we established in the case of R. v Clay, apart from the existing case law and resilience of presumption that the right to use cannabis is not "fundamental" in the sense of being generally accepted among "reasonable people"—a political stance that would seem to invite the kind of moralistic paternalism feared by Mill—there is little but legal-political convention to support prohibition on rational terms. The stalemate continues, despite the endorsement of facts such as those made by Justice McCart. Yet Young and other prominent reformers are encouraged by the eventual promise and political potency of a properly informed public to force the issue into the legislative domain. Although experienced claims makers in well-developed social movements may favour rationality as the best means to shape policy (Best 1987), where moral warrants remain unestablished, a wider range of rhetorical resources is required to appeal to 'the people,' as in the earliest stages of social problem construction. In the conclusion, following a brief overview of the study and arguments presented in this book, I will discuss some central implications of the findings and offer closing general remarks.

## CONCLUSION

Following a contextual constructionist (Best 1989, 1993) approach to social problems inquiry, this research looked at the rhetorical strategies employed in a study of drug reform claims making, with specific reference to the 'marijuana problem.' By examining strengths and weaknesses of discursive practices in relation to political arrangements, and the public forums where drug issues are debated, I have extended the constructionist focus on claims making toward a more openly critical mode of inquiry. Evaluating the rhetorical features of claims making is by its very nature subjective, and I acknowledge the extent to which my own value commitments have influenced my judgement in reaching these conclusions. To summarize my argument, despite the short term political advantages of using harm reduction as a strategic "stepping stone" to broader reform based on human rights principles, in the long run there are problems with forgoing moral warrants in favour of more 'rational' value-neutral arguments.

In claiming a middle-ground approach to drug problems, the latter stance conveys a tacit acceptance of the very endangerment themes that uphold drug prohibition. As a consequence, counter-rhetorical strategies that integrate themes of "entitlement" (Ibarra and Kitsuse 1993) are precluded inviting cooption by forces inconsistent with harm reduction's founding principles of tolerance and respect for human rights. Harm reduction's one-sided focus on harm also precludes any serious consideration of substance use having a variety of benefits. Considering only the harms due to drug use, at the exclusion of possible benefits, reinforces and reproduces prohibitionist interpretations of the balance of power between drugs and the human will. Offering no direct challenge to the exaggerated drug slave analogies and fears of many status quo defenders, harm reduction disregards its underlying respect for autonomous choice and the rights of the person.

Nadelmann (1993) contends the greatest challenge for harm reduction lies in the promotion of its underlying ideals. These ideals, I have suggested, are intimately connected with the respect for human rights and norms of social tolerance behind the rights-centred morality of modern western culture. With appeal to the assertion of basic human rights under constitutional democracy in Canada, I develop moral warrants serving as a "beachhead" (Best 1987) of accepted principles from which the need for law reform must be ultimately argued. With widespread informal tolerance of possession and use of marijuana in Canada and elsewhere, harm reduction measures for cannabis are already developing in practice in many jurisdictions. Actual changes in policy, however, remain ever elusive due to the a stalemate that, despite all the evidence to the contrary, continues to define all use in terms of endangerment and thereby requiring coercive control.

Hope for the future prospects of reform though in this study was encouraged on the basis of the potential potency of a properly informed public, and further development of critical rhetorical resources integrating moral-rational approaches to claims making. It was argued that strict rationality is irrational because purely rational arguments are immobilizing. Attending to rhetorical dimensions of claims making suggests accepted standards of rationality will vary. Emphasizing rights and freedom of expression was a mainstay of the activists and lawyers in this study. Harm reduction arguments were more commonly presented by the academic drug policy observers. Human rights based claims flow from explicit moral standards. By contrast, harm reduction arguments are avowedly amoral, or morally neutral, in character. Maintaining strictly scientific standards of rationality, however, is an ideal seldom realized in practice. All of my informants were more or less accepting of liberal assumptions of entitlement, despite the tendency of some of them to downplay moral warrants.

As experienced claims makers seeking to redefine a well-established social problem, their projected standards of rationality reflect professional and disciplinary training and related boundaries that shape the claims they make. I have argued that strategic moral grounding in supportive rhetorical traditions has been compromised at times by those who have adopted a middle-ground approach. To transcend the technocratic rhetoric of science and its complement of western bureaucratic "professionalism" (see Hariman 1989), a subjective value commitment is not only forgivable but indispensable for effective claims making by drug policy observers. Social scientists operating in public policy arenas need not hesitate to explicate their values as belonging or related to the emancipatory projects of left-liberal academics. The much maligned liberal tradition and label, from which many professionals today feel obliged to disassociate, asserts a moral commitment that is as established and viable, if not more so in our culture, as concessions to maintaining the prohibitionist mentality that has been codified in laws that target *some* drugs and their users.

According to Richards (1982), the contention that drug use experience should not be protected by constitutional principles of tolerance is not an argument, but rather the expression of a long standing tradition of public morality—a tradition that, failing to observe constitutional constraints on the kind of harm that may be the object of criminal penalties, is inconsistent with deeper constitutional values. Appeals to a common morality, expressing the very contempt for autonomy that should trigger appropriate constitutional attack and remedy, cannot be sustained, he continues: "...higher-order interests in freedom and rationality would identify respect for choices to use drugs as an aspect of personal dignity that is worthy of protection...by courts and legislatures" (Richards 1982, p. 187). Further, calling for a logical division of labour in the process of claims making for drug policy reform, Richards argued that the courts might move more aggressively in the case of marijuana, where the argument for decriminalization seems very clear and the case for extensive regulation is weak. Legislatures might be more appropriately called upon where, in addition to decriminalization, an extensive regulatory scheme may be required (as in cases such as of heroin maintenance, for example).

To say that a person has a human right to use drugs is not to assert that such a right should be exercised. To assert the existence of such a right is rather to make a legal-political claim that the conduct must be protected from coercive prohibition by the state. Respect for the right to use drugs preserves individual experience from a cultural hegemony rooted in an absolutist conception of public morality that fails to take seriously modern western ideals of human rights and freedoms and social tolerance allowing a plurality of perspectives. The drug law enforcement bureaucracy seeks to trivialize these values by demanding our "simplistic subservience to technological civilization" (Richards 1982, p. 188). In their interpretations of the fundamental principles of justice that are accepted among reasonable people, North American court decisions have continued to fail to uphold the right to use cannabis as a freedom of importance to warrant constitutional protection. Such a conclusion, implying a common public morality that is shared by all good citizens, reinforces the distinction between *positive liberty* and rights-centred *negative liberties* that do not fall within the agreed upon range of protected actions.

This may be inconsistent with the respect for human rights and social tolerance embodied in the *Charter*; however, the assumption that if such a right is not already protected it must be too trivial to warrant constitutional attention is backed by the full weight of legal-political convention. Effectively challenging the protectionist tendencies that stand in the way of the drug reform movement is ultimately contingent on

131

advancing human rights claims providing a foundation for moral-rational appeals. This approach gives proper weight to challenges against presumed notions of the common good in favour of more liberal interpretations of the freedoms provided in the *Charters* of Canada and other constitutional democracies. Returning briefly to the relevance of critical inquiries concerning social movements and the influence of media, it is argued that in bureaucratically administered societies the mainstream media reflects the dominant ideology in the face of cultural pluralism (Ericson, Baranek, and Chan 1987). The dominant culture, notes Gusfield (1981, p. 30; see also Bauman 1976), "...consists of turning everything which is not inevitable into the improbable, effectively eliminating alternatives to itself."

When private knowledge as widespread as marijuana use so blatantly contradicts media treatment of the subject, however, the dominant culture of fear is also becoming deconstructed and transformed via media as public knowledge is increasingly derived from private knowledge. The expansion of alternative media resources, and growing number of participants in social policy debates, means that sociological understandings of the media (e.g., that focus on its role as a deviance designator, reinforcing hegemonic definitions of drug problems) may be in need of substantial revision. With increasing media literacy, social differentiation, and segmentation among audiences, the reality of dealing with diversity in a heterogeneous society means that new public knowledge is increasingly filtered into the mainstream mass media through less conventional media sources. This "multi-mediated" reality (McRobbie and Thornton 1995), among other possibilities and theoretical contentions beyond our present scope, challenges the mainstream selectivity of sources informing public knowledge in drug policy debates (see Shepherd 1981).

The rhetoric of science backing status quo assumptions in this process is subjected to ever greater competition from alternative sources of knowledge and opinion. As the misappropriation of scientific knowledge in service of the dominant order encounters greater competition from these "disorderly zones of activity" (Shotter 1989), a rhetorically conscious social science provides a critical alternative enabling rival formulations to be publicly competitive and accessible through media. Bollinger (1997) established the importance of disorderly activity with reference to cannabis reform. Citing the "almost uncountable sub-legal realms of reform" presented by internal resistance to maintaining U.S. style drug policies in Europe, he argues: "...the existing heterogeneity and even chaos in actual cannabis control paradoxically enhances possibilities for a slow but constructive evolution away from harsh repression" (p. 12). Most importantly perhaps, disorderly debate via media provides a public forum that facilitates the bridging of moral

132

and rational discourse suggested in this book.

Whereas arguments contradicting the dominant order are generally disadvantaged in mainstream media, these must be contended with so long as they are 'out there;' and they are more difficult to dismiss outright once they become organized and active in the political process. A noteworthy illustration that informed the present study, concerns a two-page ad in the New York Times (June 8, 1998: A12-13), coinciding with a UN meeting on drug policy, which publicized the names of 500 prominent signatories that endorsed a call for ending the "global war on drugs" because it causes more harm than substance use itself. Such a bold public statement, though of no actual force and effect with respect to the priorities of the United Nations (which instead renewed commitment to the pursuit of a "drug-free planet" through prohibition and intensified eradication efforts), lent an unprecedented level of legitimacy to drug reform as being no longer such a radical or fringe idea that can be so easily ignored by our ruling institutions.

The "essentially contested" (Gallie 1962) nature of the drug war is evident in the statuses imputed to its challengers. On the side of order, the status quo defenders oppose licentious 'liberals' who would have us tolerate all drug use and accommodate addiction in the name of 'harm reduction.' In response to the foregoing anti-drug war declaration, General McCaffery released a public statement, for example, warning that: "There is a carefully camouflaged, exorbitantly funded, well-heeled, elitist group whose ultimate goal is to legalize drug use in the U.S." (Ottawa Citizen: June 29, 1998). Whereas few drug law critics favour legalization, the indiscriminate grouping of drug policy reformers under one, albeit misrepresented, "liberal" label may unwittingly contribute to the rhetorical coherence and advancement of a movement promoting publicly accessible moral warrants for change.

Bringing together moral and rational resources, through the repetition and reinterpretation of liberalism as a "living tradition" (Bellah et al. 1985), draws attention to consistencies between opposing sides, refocusing disputes, and evolving new traditions. As "theory in practice" (Shotter 1993), the called for convergence has greater cumulative potential for supplanting outmoded principles that are resistant to change. The essentially contested nature of conditions and arguments presented here ensure endless competition between rivals with no general methods or principles for deciding among possibilities. The very nature of the rivalry is such that "...each group's claim to have a better line than its rivals, only makes sense *in relation* to the claims of their rivals, and is developed as a counter to them" (Shotter 1989, p. 159, italics in original). To use an essentially contested concept is to use it *against* other uses, seeking not to end the competition through

133

elimination of one's rivals but to continue to adapt and participate *with them*.

Invoking the spirit of modern liberalism in terms of a living tradition cannot provide a ready-made solution to this or any other moral problem. Rather it facilitates a continuous process of reinterpretation, further articulation, and refinement, assuming the authority of moral tradition to publicly pursue these aims as a common project. Such problems are only problems in the sense that they are essentially contested, giving rise to endless disputes sustained by perfectly respectable arguments and evidence on both sides of the issue; they will continue to be interminably debated for as long as there are free-willed persons able to debate them, not because they are in any sense resolvable. Tracing the development of western social movements more generally, Starr (1985) draws on the Weberian (1956) distinction between formal and substantive rationality. Whereas the culture of bureaucracy is rooted in the former, freedom is founded on "substantive rationality" which has its basis in values.

In claims making groups with diffuse social boundaries (as in the current movement for marijuana law reform in Canada and other constitutional democracies) there is a particular need for ideology, he continues, which "...links the present to the future, engenders commitment, and motivates action in a way that objective science cannot" (p. 320). Advancing the debate in terms of "humanist reason" (Starr 1985) means striving for the synthesis of rationality and moral community and evolving corresponding rights and freedoms in accordance with pragmatic social planning and policy. The approach called for here is concerned with the promotion of relationships and values reflecting the norms of social tolerance and personal autonomy found in western conceptions of liberal morality. A rhetorically conscious social science, it is argued, provides a critical alternative to the dominant order by making rival formulations publicly accessible. Engendering commitment to more meaningful reform, in the context of new century drug policy claims making, means openly acknowledging the moral impetus for action that makes rationality more relevant in this and other areas of critical inquiry, contemporary social problems research and debates.

## BIBLIOGRAPHY

Alexander, B.K. Peaceful Measures: Canada's Way Out of the "War on Drugs." University of Toronto Press, 1990.

Anderson, P. High in America: The True Story Behind NORML and the Politics of Marijuana. New York: Viking Press, 1981.

Aronson, N. "Science as a Claims-making Activity," Pp. 1-30 in Schneider, J.W. and Kitsuse, J.I. (eds.), Studies in the Sociology of Social Problems. Norwood, N.J.: Ablex, 1984.

Beauchesne, L. "Social Morality and the Civil Rights of Canadian Drug Users," Journal of Drug Issues, 21(1), 1991, 165-182.

Becker, H.S. "Becoming a Marihuana User," American Journal of Sociology, 59, 1953, 235-242.

————. "A Note on Interviewing Tactics," Human Organization, 12, Winter 1954, 31-32.

————. "Marihuana Use and Social Control," Social Problems, 3, 1955, 35-44.

————. "Problems of Inference and Proof in Participant Observation," American Sociological Review, 23, December 1958, 652-660.

————. Outsiders: Studies in the Sociology of Deviance. New York: Free Press, 1963.

————. "History, Culture, and Subjective Experience: An Exploration of the Social Bases of Drug-Induced Experiences," Journal of Health and Social Behavior, 8, 1967, 163-176.

————. Sociological Work: Method and Substance. Chicago: Aldine, 1970.

————. "Herbert Blumer's Conceptual Impact," Symbolic Interaction, 11(1), 1988, 13-21.

Bellah, R.N., Madsen, R., Sullivan, W.A., Swidler, A., and Tipton, S.M. Habits of the Heart: Individualism and Commitment in American Life. Berkeley: University of California Press, 1985.

Berger, P.L. and Luckmann, T. The Social Construction of Reality: A Treatise in the Sociology of Knowledge. New York: Doubleday, 1966.

Best, J. "Rhetoric in Claims-Making: Constructing the Missing Children Problem," Social Problems, 34(2), 1987, 101-121.

————. "Afterword," Pp. 243-253 in Images of Issues: Typifying Contemporary Social Problems. New York: Aldine de Gruyter, 1989.

————. "But Seriously Folks: The Limitations of the Strict Constructionist Interpretation of Social Problems," Pp. 109-127 in G. Miller and J.A. Holstein (eds.) Constructionalist Controversies. N.J.: Aldine, 1993.

————. Images of Issues: Typifying Contemporary Social Problems, 2nd ed. New York: Aldine de Gruyter, 1995.

Bindman, S. "Unelected Judges: Should They Make the Law?" Hamilton Spectator, January 10, 1998, C1,C6.

Blackwell, J., Green, M., and Solomon, R. "Cannabis Control Policy: A Discussion Paper," Unpublished research study, Health Promotion Branch, Department of Health and Welfare: Ottawa, 1979.

Blumer, H. "Social Problems as Collective Behavior," Social Problems, 18, 1971, 298-306.

Blumstein, A. "Making Rationality Relevant," Criminology, 31(1), 1993, 1-16.

Bollinger, L. Cannabis Science: From Prohibition to Human Right. New York: Peter Lang Inc., 1997.

Bonnie, R.C. and Whitebread, C. The Marihuana Conviction. Charlottesville: University Press of Virginia, 1974.

Boyd, N. High Society: Legal and Illegal Drugs in Canada. Toronto: Key Porter, 1991.

Buning, E. "Harm Reduction and Health Promotion," workshop presentation, Fifth International Conference on the Reduction of Drug-related Harm, Toronto, March 1993.

Canadian Charter of Rights and Freedoms. Part I of the Constitution Act, 1982, being Schedule B to the Canada Act, 1982 (U.K.), c. 11.

CCSA. "Substance Abuse Policy in Canada," Presentation to the House Standing Committee on Health. Ottawa: Canadian Centre on Substance Abuse, 1997.

Chambliss, W.J. Crime and the Legal Process. New York: McGraw-Hill, 1969.

————. "Toward a Political Economy of Crime," Theory and Society, 2, 1975, 149-170.

————. "The State and Criminal Law," in W.J. Chambers and M. Mankoff (eds.) Whose Law? What Order: A Conflict Approach to Criminology. New York: John Wiley & Sons, 1976.

Cohen, J. "Achieving a Reduction in Drug-Related Harm Through Education," in N. Heather, A. Wodak, and E. Nadelmann (eds.) Psychoactive Drugs and Harm Reduction: From Faith to Science. London: Whurr Publishers, 1993.

Cohen, P. and Sas, A. "Cannabis Use, A Stepping Stone to Other Drugs? The Case of Amsterdam," Pp. 49-82 in L. Bollinger (ed.) Cannabis Science: From Prohibition to Human Right. New York: Peter Lang, Inc., 1997.

Cook, S.J. "Canadian Narcotics Legislation, 1908-1923: A Conflict Model Interpretation," Canadian Review of Sociology and Anthropology, 6, 1969, 36-46.

Corbin, J. and Strauss, A. "Grounded Theory Research: Procedures, Canons, and Evaluative Criteria," Qualitative Sociology, 13(1), 1990, 3-21.

Czubaroff, J. "The Deliberative Character of Strategic Scientific Debates," Pp. 28-47 in H.W. Simons (ed.) Rhetoric in the Human Sciences. London: Sage, 1989.

Denzin, N.K. The Research Act. Chicago: Aldine, 1970.

Devlin, P. The Enforcement of Morals. London: Oxford University Press, 1965.

DiChiara, A. and Galliher, J.F. "Dissonance and Contradictions in the Origins of Marihuana Decriminalization," Law & Society Review, 28(1), 1994, 41-77.

Dickson, D.T. "Bureaucracy and Morality," Social Problems, 16, Fall 1968, 143-156.

Dupont, R.L. Getting Tough on Gateway Drugs: A Guide for the Family. Washington DC: American Psychiatric Press Inc., 1985.

Ebin, D. (ed.) The Drug Experience. New York: Orion Press, 1961.

Erickson, P.G. Cannabis Criminals: The Social Effects of Punishment on Drug Users. Toronto: Addiction Research Foundation, 1980.

————. "Prospects of Harm Reduction for Psychostimulants," Pp. 184-210 in N. Heather, A. Wodak, and E. Nadelmann (eds.) Psychoactive Drugs and Harm Reduction: From Faith to Science. London: Whurr Publishers, 1993.

————. "The Harm Minimization Option for Cannabis: History and Prospects in Canadian Drug Policy," in L. Harrison and J. Inciardi (eds.) Harm Reduction. Sage Publications, 1997a.

————. "Reducing the Harm of Adolescent Substance Use," Canadian Medical Association Journal, 156(10), 1997b, 1397-1399.

————. "Neglected and Rejected: A Case Study of the Impact of Social Research on Canadian Drug Policy," Canadian Journal of Sociology, 23, 1998, 263-280.

Erickson, P.G. and Smart, R. "The LeDain Commission Recommendations," Pp. 100-108 in S. Einstein (ed.) The Community's Response to Drug Use. New York: Pergamon Press, 1980.

Ericson, R.V., Baranek, P.M., and Chan, J.B.L. Visualizing Deviance: A Study of News Organization. University of Toronto Press, 1987.

Fromberg, E. "Prohibition as a Necessary Stage in the Acculturation of Foreign Drugs," Pp. 127-136 in N. Heather, A. Wodak, and E. Nadelmann (eds.) Psychoactive Drugs and Harm Reduction: From Faith to Science. London: Whurr Publishers, 1993.

Gallie, W.B. "Essentially Contested Concepts," Pp. 121-146 in M. Black (ed.) The Importance of Language. N.J.: Prentice-Hall, 1962.

Gamson, W.A. Talking Politics. Cambridge University Press, 1992.

Giffen, P.J., Endicott, S., and Lambert, S. Panic and Indifference: The Politics of Canada's Drug Laws. Ottawa: Canadian Centre for Substance Abuse, 1991.

Glaser, B. and Strauss, A. The Discovery of Grounded Theory: Strategies for Qualitative Research. Chicago: Aldine, 1967.

Goode, E. and Ben-Yehuda, N. Moral Panics: The Social Construction of Deviance. Cambridge, MA: Blackwell, 1994.

Gould, A. "Sweden's Syringe Exchange Debate: Moral Panic in a Rational Society," Journal of Social Policy, 23(2), 1994, 195-217.

Gouldner, A.W. "The Sociologist as Partisan: Sociology and the Welfare State," American Sociologist, May 1968, 103-116.

Gray, H. "Cultural Theory, Social Construction, and Social Problems," Pp. 193-205 in G. Miller and J.A. Holstein (eds.) Constructionalist Controversies. N.J.: Aldine, 1993.

Gusfield, J.R. Symbolic Crusade: Status Politics and the American Temperance Movement. Urbana Ill.: University of Illinois Press, 1963.

————. "The (F)utility of Knowledge?: The Relation of Social Science to Public Policy toward Drugs," Annals of the American Academy of Political and Social Science, 417, 1975, 1-15.

————. The Culture of Public Problems: Drinking-Driving and the Symbolic Order. Chicago: University of Chicago Press, 1981.

————. "Theories and Hobgoblins," SSSP Newsletter, 17, Fall 1985, 16-18.

————. "The Control of Drinking and Driving in the United States: A Period of Transition?" Pp.109-135 in M.D. Laurence, J.R. Snortum, and F.E. Zimring (eds.) Social Control of the Drinking Driver. University of Chicago Press, 1988.

Hariman, R. "The Rhetoric of Inquiry and the Professional Scholar," Pp. 211-232 in H.W. Simons (ed.) Rhetoric in the Human Sciences. London: Sage, 1989.

Hart, H.L.A. Law, Liberty and Morality. Stanford, CA: Stanford University Press, 1963.

Hathaway, A.D. "Marijuana and Tolerance: Revisiting Becker's Sources of Control," Deviant Behavior, 18 (2), 1997a, 103-124.

————. "Marijuana and Lifestyle: Exploring Tolerable Deviance," Deviant Behavior, 18(3), 1997b, 213-232.

Hawks, D. "Impediments to the Global Adoption of Harm-reduction Policies," Pp. 93-102 in N. Heather, A. Wodak, and E. Nadelmann (eds.) Psychoactive Drugs and Harm Reduction: From Faith to Science. London: Whurr Publishers, 1993.

Helmer, J. Drugs and Minority Oppression. New York: Seabury, 1975.

Himmelstein, J.L. "Drug Politics Theory: Analysis and Critique," Journal of Drug Issues, 8, 1978, 37-52.

Ibarra, P.R. and Kitsuse, J.I. "Vernacular Constituents of Moral Discourse: An Interactionist Proposal for the Study of Social Problems," Pp. 21-54 in G. Miller and J.A. Holstein (eds.) Constructionalist Controversies. N.J.: Aldine, 1993.

Jenks, S.M. "An Analysis of Risk Reduction Among Organized Groups that Promote Marijuana and Psychedelic Drugs," Journal of Drug Issues, 25(3), 1995, 629-647.

Johnson, G. and Newmeyer, J. "Pleasure, Punishment and Moral Indignation," Sociology and Social Research, 59(2), 1975, 82-95.

Kandel, D.B., Yamaguchi, K., and Chen, K. "Stages of Progression in Drug Involvement from Adolescence to Adulthood: Further Evidence for the Gateway Theory," Journal of Studies on Alcohol, September 1992, 447-457.

Kandel, D.B. and Yamaguchi, K. "From Beer to Crack: Development Patterns of Drug Involvement," American Journal of Public Health, 83(6), 1993, 851-855.

Kant, I. Foundations of the Metaphysics of Morals. 1785. (L.W. Beck trans.) Indianapolis, Ind.: Bobbs-Merrill Company, Inc., 1959.

Kaplan, J. Marijuana: The New Prohibition. New York: Meridian, 1971.

Kingdon, J.W. Agendas, Alternatives, and Public Policies, 2nd ed. Boston: Little, Brown & Co., 1995.

LeDain, G. Cannabis: A Report of the Commission of Inquiry into the Non-medical Use of Drugs. Ottawa: Information Canada, 1972.

Lemert, E.M. Social Pathology. New York: McGraw-Hill, 1951.

Liazos, A. "The Poverty of the Sociology of Deviance: Nuts, Sluts, and Perverts," Social Problems, 20, Summer 1973, 103-126.

Lindesmith, A. Opiate Addiction. Evanston, Ill.: Principia Press, 1947.

————. The Addict and the Law. New York: Random House, 1965.

————. Addiction and the Opiates. Chicago: Aldine, 1968.

Lowi, T.J. The End of Liberalism. New York: Norton, 1969.

MacIntyre, A. Whose Justice? Which Rationality? University of Notre Dame Press, 1988.

McCarthy, J.D. "Activists, Authorities, and Media Framing of Drunk Driving," Pp. 133-167 in E. Larana, H. Johnston, and J.R. Gusfield (eds.) New Social Movements: From Ideology to Identity. Philadelphia: Temple University Press, 1994.

McRobbie, A. and Thornton, S.L. "Rethinking 'Moral Panic' for Multi-mediated Social Worlds," British Journal of Sociology, 46, 1995, 559-574.

Mill, J.S. On Liberty. London, 1859.

————. Utilitarianism. London, 1863.

Miller, G. Enforcing the Work Ethic: Rhetoric and Everyday Life in a Work Incentive Program. New York: State University of New York Press, 1991.

Mitchell, C.N. "A Justice-based Argument for the Uniform Regulation of Psychoactive Drugs," Pp. 407-443 in J.C. Blackwell and P.G. Erickson (eds.) Illicit Drugs in Canada: A Risky Business. Nelson Canada, 1988.

————. The Drug Solution. Carleton University Press, 1990.

Morgan, J.P., Riley, D., and Chesher, G.B. "Cannabis: Legal Reform, Medicinal Use and Harm Reduction," Pp. 211-229 in N. Heather, A. Wodak, and E. Nadelmann (eds.) Psychoactive Drugs and Harm Reduction: From Faith to Science. London: Whurr Publishers, 1993.

Moynihan, D.P. "The War Against the Automobile," Public Interest, 3, 1966, 10-26.

Mugford, S. "Harm Reduction: Does it Lead Where its Proponents Imagine?" Pp. 21-33 in N. Heather, A. Wodak, and E. Nadelmann (eds.) Psychoactive Drugs and Harm Reduction: From Faith to Science. London: Whurr Publishers, 1993.

Murphy, E. The Black Candle. Toronto: Thomas Allen, 1922.

Musto, D.F. The American Disease: Origins of Narcotic Control. New Haven: Yale University Press, 1973.

Nadelmann, E.A. "Progressive Legalizers, Progressive Prohibitionists and the Reduction of Drug-Related Harm," Pp. 34-45 in N. Heather, A. Wodak, and E. Nadelmann (eds.) Psychoactive Drugs and Harm Reduction: From Faith to Science. London: Whurr Publishers, 1993.

Nader, R. Unsafe at Any Speed: The Designed-In Dangers of the American Automobile, Updated ed. New York: Grossman Books, 1972.

Nahas, G.G. Keep Off the Grass. Middlebury, VT: P.S. Eriksson, 1990.

National Organization for the Reform of Marijuana Laws (NORML). "The Responsibilities of Marijuana Use," NORML's Active Resistance, 1(1), 1993, 10.

Poulin, C. and Elliott, D. "Alcohol, Tobacco and Cannabis Use Among Nova Scotia Adolescents: Implications for Prevention and Harm Reduction," Canadian Medical Association Journal, 156(10), 1997, 1387-1393.

Pross, J.P. "Pressure Groups: Adaptive Instruments of Political Communication," Pp. 1-26 in Pressure Group Behavior in Canadian Politics. Toronto: McGraw-Hill Ryerson, 1975.

Puder, G. Crossfire: A Street Cop's Stand Against Violence, Corruption and the War on Drugs. Toronto: Douglas & McIntyre, 1999.

Quinney, R. Crime and Justice in Society. Boston: Little, Brown, 1969.

————. The Social Reality of Crime. Boston: Little, Brown, 1970.

————. Critique of Legal Order. Boston: Little, Brown, 1974.

————. Criminology: Analysis and Critique of Crime in America. Boston: Little, Brown, 1975.

————. Class, State and Crime. New York: David McKay, 1977.

Rafter, N. "Some Consequences of Strict Constructionism," Social Problems, 39(1), 1992, 38-39.

Rainwater, L. and Pittman, D.J. "Ethical Problems in Studying a Politically Sensitive and Deviant Community," Social Problems, 14, 1967, 357-366.

Reasons, C. "The Politics of Drugs: An Inquiry in the Sociology of Social Problems," Sociological Quarterly, 15, Summer 1974, 381-404.

Redekop, B. "Pot Smokers Second-Class Citizens: Lawyer," Winnipeg Free Press, January 5, 1995, B2.

Reeves, J.L. and Campbell, R. Cracked Coverage: Television News, the Anti-Cocaine Coverage, and the Reagan Legacy. Durham, N.C.: Duke University Press, 1994.

Reinarman, C. "The Social Construction of An Alcohol Problem: The Case of Mothers Against Drunk Drivers and Social Control in the 1980s," Theory and Society, 17, 1988, 91-119.

Reinarman, C. and Levine H.G. "Crack Attack: America's Latest Drug Scare, 1986-1992," Pp. 147-186 in J. Best (ed.) Images of Issues: Typifying Contemporary Social Problems. New York: Aldine de Gruyter, 1995.

Richards, D.A.J. "Human Rights and Moral Ideals: An Essay on the Moral Theory of Liberalism," Social Theory and Practice, 5(3-4), 1979, 461-488.

————. Sex, Drugs, Death and the Law: An Essay on Human Rights and Overcriminalization. Totowa, N.J.: Rowman and Littlefield, 1982.

Riley, D. The Harm Reduction Model. Toronto: Harm Reduction Network Printing, 1996.

Robbe, H.W.J. "Cannabis and Car Driving," Pp. 127-137 in L. Bollinger (ed.) Cannabis Science: From Prohibition to Human Right. New York: Peter Lang, Inc., 1997.

Rose, A.M. "A Research Note on Interviewing," American Journal of Sociology, 51, September 1945, 143-144.

Sarbin, T.R. and Kitsuse, J.I. "A Prologue to Constructing the Social," Pp. 1-18 in Constructing the Social. Thousand Oaks, CA: Sage, 1994.

Scheerer, S. "The New Dutch and German Drug Laws: Social and Political Conditions for Successful Criminalization and Decriminalization," Law & Society Review, 12, 1978, 585-606.

Schneider, J.W. "Defining the Definitional Perspective on Social Problems," Social Problems, 32, 1985a, 232-234.

————. "Social Problems Theory: The Constructionist View," Annual Review of Sociology, 11, 1985b, 209-229.

Schur, E.M. Drug Addiction in America and England. Bloomington, Ind.: Indiana University Press, 1964.

————. Crimes Without Victims. Englewood Cliffs, N.J.: Prentice-Hall, 1965.

Schwandt, T. "Constructivist, Interpretivist Approaches to Human Inquiry," Pp. 118-137 in N. Denzin and T. Lincoln (eds.) Handbook of Qualitative Research. Thousand Oaks: Sage, 1994.

Schwartz, M.A. "Politics and Moral Causes in Canada and the United States," Comparative Social Research, 4, 1981, 65-90.

————. "Comparing United States and Canadian Public Policy: A Review of Strategies," Policy Studies Journal, 14(4), 1986, 566-575.

Shedler, J. and Block, J. "Adolescent Drug Use and Psychological Health: A Longitudinal Inquiry," American Psychologist, 45(5), 1990, 612-630.

Shepherd, R.G. "Selectivity of Sources: Reporting the Marijuana Controversy," Journal of Communication, Spring 1981, 129-137.

Shotter, J. "Rhetoric and the Recovery of Civil Society," Economy and Society, 18(2), 1989, 149-166.

————. Cultural Politics of Everyday Life. University of Toronto Press, 1993.

Signorile, V. "Buridan's Ass: The Statistical Rhetoric of Science and the Problem of Equiprobability," Pp. 69-88 in H.W. Simons (ed.) Rhetoric in the Human Sciences. London: Sage, 1989.

Single, E. "The Impact of Marijuana Decriminalization: An Update," Journal of Public Health Policy, 10(4), 1989, 456-466.

————. "The Concept of Harm Reduction and its Application to Alcohol: The 6th Dorothy Black Lecture," Drugs: Education, Prevention and Policy, 4(1), 1997, 7-22.

Single, E. and Tocher, B. "Legislating Responsible Alcohol Service: An Inside View of the New Liquor Licence Act of Ontario," British Journal of Addiction, 87, 1992, 1433-1443.

Single, E., Conley, P., Hewitt, D., Mitic, W., Poulin, C., Riley, D., Room, R., Sawka, E., and Topp, J. "Harm Reduction: Concepts and Practice—A Policy Discussion Paper," CCSA National Working Group on Policy. Ottawa: Canadian Centre on Substance Abuse, 1995.

Skolnick, J.H. and Dombrink, J. "The Legalization of Deviance," Criminology, 16(2), 1978, 193-208.
143

Solomon, R. "The Noble Pursuit of Evil: Arrest, Search, and Seizure in Canadian Drug Law," Pp. 263-290 in J.C. Blackwell and P.G. Erickson (eds.) Illicit Drugs in Canada: A Risky Business. Nelson Canada, 1988.

Solomon, R., Single, E., and Erickson P.G. "Legal Considerations in Canadian Cannabis Policy," Canadian Public Policy, 9(4), 1983, 419-433.

Spector, M. "Learning to Study Public Figures," Pp. 98-109 in W.B. Shaffir, R.A. Stebbins, and A. Turowetz (eds.) Fieldwork Experience: Qualitative Approaches to Social Research. New York: St. Martins Press, 1980.

Spector, M. and Kitsuse, J.I. Constructing Social Problems. Menlo Park: Cummings, 1977.

————. Constructing Social Problems, 2nd ed. Hawthorne, N.Y.: Aldine de Gruyter, 1987.

Starr, J. Cultural Politics: Radical Movements in Modern History. New York: Praeger, 1985.

Strang, J. "Drug Use and Harm Reduction: Responding to the Challenge," Pp. 3-20 in N. Heather, A. Wodak, and E. Nadelmann (eds.) Psychoactive Drugs and Harm Reduction: From Faith to Science. London: Whurr Publishers, 1993.

Strauss, A. and Corbin, J. "Grounded Theory Methodology: An Overview," Pp. 273-285 in N. Denzin and T. Lincoln (eds.) Handbook of Qualitative Research. Thousand Oaks: Sage, 1994.

Szasz, T. Our Right to Drugs: The Case for a Free Market. New York: Praeger, 1992.

Taylor, I. (ed.) Critical Criminology. London: Routledge and Kegan Paul, 1975.

Taylor, I., Walton, P., and Young, J. The New Criminology. London: Routledge and Kegan Paul, 1973.

Teevan, J. "Subjective Perception of Deterrence," Journal of Research in Crime and Delinquency, 13(2), 1976, 155-164.

Toulmin, S.E. The Uses of Argument. Cambridge University Press, 1958.

Turk, A.T. Criminality and Legal Order. Chicago: Rand McNally, 1969.

Weber, M. The Theory of Social and Economic Organization. (A.M. Henderson and T. Parsons trans.) Glencoe, Ill.: The Free Press, 1956.

Weppner, R.S. and Inciardi, J.A. "Decriminalizing Marijuana," International Journal of Offender Therapy and Comparative Criminology, 22(2), 1978, 115-126.

Wong, D.B. Moral Relativity. University of California Press, 1984.

Woolgar, S. and Pawluch D. "Ontological Gerrymandering: The Anatomy of Social Problems Explanations," Social Problems, 32(2), 1985, 214-227.

Zimmer, L. and Morgan, J.P. Marijuana Myths Marijuana Facts: A Review of the Scientific Evidence. New York: The Lindesmith Center, 1997.

Zinberg, N.E. Drug, Set, and Setting: The Basis for Controlled Intoxicant Use. New Haven, Connecticut: Yale University Press, 1984.

CPSIA information can be obtained at www.ICGtesting.com
Printed in the USA
241548LV00009B/66/P